AMSTERDAM ARCHITECTURE
A Guide

Edited by Guus Kemme

Photographs by Jan Derwig

Gaston Bekkers
Paul Broers
Judikje Kiers
Marga van Klinken
Wilfred van Leeuwen
Birgitte de Maar
Erik Mattie
Renate Meijer
Jouke van de Werf

Fourth expanded and revised edition

 UITGEVERIJ THOTH

Acknowledgments

I would like to take the opportunity of the publication of this guide to thank first of all Jan Derwig for his support. Apart from taking all the photographs he has given a vast amount of advice in the creation of this guide.
I would also like to thank Paul Broers, Judikje Kiers, Marga van Klinken, Wilfred van Leeuwen, Erik Mattie and Jouke van der Werf for the immense energy with which they have collected information and written the texts.
I am indebted to all contributors for their advice on the selection of subjects covered; especially to Dirk Baalman of the Vrije Universiteit, Amsterdam, Dick van Woerkom of the Nederlands Documentatiecentrum voor de Bouwkunst and Henk Zantkuyl of the Gemeentelijk Bureau Monumentenzorg, Amsterdam.
Finally, my thanks to the publisher, Kees van den Hoek, for making this venture possible and for a most pleasant association.
The combined efforts of all these people have made it possible to create a guide which, in word and image, presents an outline of the architectural history of the unique city of Amsterdam.

Shortly after the publication of the first edition of this guide Dick van Woerkom died, far too young. After a long career as an architect he was managing director of the Nederlands Documentatiecentrum voor de Bouwkunst (Dutch Institute for Architecture). In his own special way he stimulated many young architects and art historians. As a friend he stimulated the photographer and the editor to make this guide.

Guus Kemme

ISBN 90 6868 016 1

© 1996 Guus Kemme and THOTH Publishers, Bussum
© 1996 Photographs Jan Derwig bfn and THOTH Publishers
© Maps Dienst Openbare werken, afd. Kartografie
© Map page 114 Dienst Ruimtelijke Ordening
Photographs page 30 and 34, and nrs 157 and 227 Gemeentearchief Amsterdam
Photographs page 21, 23, 28, 29 and 37 DRO Vormgeving, Amsterdam
Photograph page 35 Gemeente Amstelveen
Photograph page 39 Fotoarchief Stadsontwikkeling, Amsterdam
Photograph page 41 Cary Markerink, Amsterdam
Photograph page 93 coll. Jan van Male, Amsterdam
Photograph nr 625 RETINA/M. Kerkhof
Photograph nr 628 Capital Press & Photo Productions bv, Amsterdam
Photograph nr 629 E. Seeder
Cover design Herwolt van Dooren
Translations Marja Kramp, Chris Gordon, Lodewijk Odé and Paul Willcox
Printing C. Haasbeek bv, Alphen aan den Rijn

Contents

Foreword

You may think: 'an architectural guide of Amsterdam', what is so spectacular about that? So much has already been written about Amsterdam, about its history, its atmosphere, the town planning and architecture. This endless row of books and articles is certainly interesting when you are sitting behind your desk or in an easy chair. Yet, if you want to know the city and its architecture, you should walk through it, look, stop and be amazed, for the richness in architecture in Amsterdam really takes you by surprise.

The urban extension of the city centre was partly a natural growth and partly planned. Yet, the major extension of the ring of concentric canals was designed both with respect to the normal, urban functions and because of aesthetic reasons.

Partly in contrast with this austerely designed urban space, but also in relation to it is the infinite variety of so many houses, the rich forms of the fanciful turrets and the hundreds of bridges.

The architecture of the city centre of Amsterdam is defined by each single house, the endless rows of ever-changing façades in the ever-bending canal walls with no ends but with surprising views. In the city centre we find a total of 21.000 houses, a third of which go back to before 1850. Each of these houses is worth a visit.

Devised by the human – *Staets* – hand in the seventeenth century, the organization of the city largely failed in the nineteenth century owing to the explosive growth in population: the Kalff plan versus the Van Niftrik plan. In the early part of this century Berlage left his stamp on Amsterdam Zuid, and Van Eesteren and Van Lohuizen gave Amsterdam its final shape with the General Development Plan (Algemeen Uitbreidingsplan, AUP). Even the controversial development of the Bijlmermeer in the sixties shows great courage.

The evolution of the design, a combination of tradition and renewal, can only be made clear by means of a chronological account. A new story has been created. This guide is a basis for many trips through this evolution, step by step, through the history of architecture. The best way to read architecture is to look, stop and be amazed. This is what this guide is for. But also as a reference book this guide has many advantages as photographs and dates are necessary for study, insight and understanding.

H.J. Zantkuyl – Gemeentelijk Bureau Monumentenzorg
D. van Woerkom – Nederlands Documentatiecentrum voor de Bouwkunst

Introduction

The great variety in the architecture of Amsterdam has often been a reason for architects, art historians or just lovers of fine buildings to pay a visit to the city. *Amsterdam Architecture* is intended as an introduction and a companion for these visitors. The chronological arrangement of the guide gives a picture of the architecture through the ages.

Amsterdam Architecture opens with an introduction to the architectural history of the city, which is followed by five seperate periods into which the history is divided. Each period includes an introduction which is followed by a great number of illustrations with the address, the name of the architect and the name and date of each building.

Although this guide can only give a limited number of examples, every effort has been made to create a picture which is as representative as possible. For those who would like to go more deeply into the subject, a list of additional examples and a comprehensive bibliography have been included. Apart from this there is a list of the bodies engaged in architectural history, the preservation of monuments and historic buildings, 'architectural walks', lectures, etc. The guide concludes with three indexes. The first of these gives a complete picture of all architects mentioned in the guide. The second and third contain the names of all the streets included in the guide and the names of the persons and the buildings respectively.

The maps on the insides of the cover-flaps show the location of the buildings illustrated in the guide. The numbers correspond to the numbers in bold face on the bottom line of the captions. This line also indicates the accessibility of the building to the public (□ = open to the public, ■ = closed to the public).

Fore more than one reason the centre of Amsterdam cannot be visited by car. The ring of concentric canals was not built to hold so many cars and the exhaust fumes are harmful to the monuments. Adequate car-parking space can be found outside the city centre and in the suburbs, from which there are good connections to the centre by public transport. It is, therefore, advisable to walk or to cycle (rent-a-bike) within the ring of concentric canals. Public transport to each of the buildings outside this ring is indicated.

*Aerial view of the Jordaan,
Prinsengracht, Keizersgracht
and Herengracht*

The history of a densely populated city

It has been said that Amsterdam is a laboratory for town-planning experiments. The creativity of a people that has to make the most of the space granted to it becomes apparent in the sequence of organic growth and conscious planning.

An aerial view of Amsterdam shows how the diversity of the various districts increases towards the perimeter. In the middle lies the famous crescent-shape of the seventeenth century concentric canals around which the ring of nineteenth century areas and, on the outskirts, the many developments of the present century, spreading far into the landscape of Noord-Holland.

Beginnings

Amsterdam is situated on the river IJ, and was built when it was not yet cut off from the Zuiderzee (renamed IJsselmeer). The river Amstel, together with the Dam, which the inhabitants built in the river around 1270, gave the town its name. A finger of land opposite the mouth of the Amstel protected the port against the westerly winds, while the tidal flow of the Zuiderzee prevented the port from silting up. The reclamation of many of the lakes surrounding the city made the thick, marshy layer of peat available for building. The buildings were all of timber, but fires in 1421 and 1453 made it essential to build in brick. To support this, long wooden piles were driven into the ground and held together by a framework. Dikes protected the land against the threatening seas but, even in the eighteenth century, were not able to prevent the farmlands from being flooded: a spectacle that scared the wits out of many a foreign visitor.

When in 1275, Amsterdam was granted exemption from paying tolls on Dutch waterways, it was able to devote itself to trade as well as to fishing. In the fourteenth and fifteenth centuries, the town became the most important port of call for many ships on their way from the German Hansa towns to Bruges, the most important trading town of the time.

The favourable position of Amsterdam and the development of small, manoeuvrable ships led to an increase in trade with the Baltic and the town itself became a permanent annual fair, at which grain and other commodities could be stored for long periods. The cargo trade and fishing stimulated industry and attracted many unemployed labourers from the countryside.

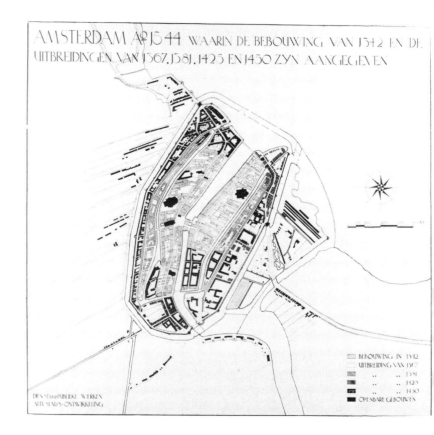

Amsterdam 1544

The first townspeople lived along the banks of the river Amstel in the Warmoesstraat and the Nieuwendijk. A wooden rampart was surrounded by the Nieuwezijds Voorburgwal and the Oudezijds Voorburgwal. In the fifteenth century the town was twice enlarged with new moats without filling up the preceding ones. The oblique dike paths became linking alleys and streets.

In 1425, when the Geldersekade and the Kloveniersburgwal in the east and the Singel in the west were built, the town was provided with its first brick fortress, with gateways, perimeter towers and round bastions. Nevertheless, the new extensions were not sufficient to cope with the increasing stream of immigrants and very soon the town literally burst at the seams. In defiance of the interests of the landowners, the inhabitants of the carpentry workshops to the east of the city, in the area around what is now the Jodenbreestraat (then known as the Lastage), demanded protection. The landowners, who were often also members of the city council, feared a drop in the price of land. In 1589, the inhabitants got what they wanted. The carpentry workshops were removed to the islands to the east of the city and the Lastage became an exclusively residential area.

The seventeenth century concentric canals

Amsterdam, which remained Roman Catholic longer than other Dutch towns, only chose the side of William of Orange during the revolt of the Northern Netherlands against the Spanish Habsburger kings (1568-1648) in 1578 when the Protestants took over the city. Amsterdam gained a reputation for freedom and tolerance. The already substantial influx of refugees grew considerably in 1585 when the powerful city of Antwerp fell into Spanish hands and was cut off from the sea. Experienced Antwerp merchants and many poor Protestants took refuge in Amsterdam and gave impetus to trade. An important contribution was also made by rich Portuguese Jews. Trade was not restricted to the Baltic and the Mediterranean; Dutch ships swarmed over the seven seas. With a fleet larger than the English, French and Spanish put together, Amsterdam became the biggest trading town and depot of the seventeenth century. The expansion of the town stimulated the establishment of whale-oil factories, ship-yards, soap works, textile industry and many other industries and gave rise to financial institutions such as the banks and the stock exchange.

Recruiting cheap labour became more important for the landowning merchants and entrepreneurs than land speculation. Between 1570 and 1640, the population had increased from 30.000 to 139.000. It is clear that the decision of 1609 to undertake a considerable expansion of the city had been absolutely essential. All remaining open spaces were built on and former monasteries were requisitioned for public services. Increasing prosperity resulted in increasing social differences.

Citizens who had become rich wished to live far away from the smell of the docks and the noise of the warehouses. This wish had to be taken into consideration in the new development. The western section of the new expansion, as far as the Leidsegracht, was completed between 1612 and 1625 and the eastern expansion was commenced in 1658. The ramparts, with 26 bastions, were laid out like a barbed chain around the city. Of the old city gates, only the Sint Antoniespoort remained and the old city towers were provided with spires. New gateways appeared on the exit roads to Haarlem, Leiden, Utrecht, Weesp and Muiden.

Within the city walls, the western part was parcelled out in two ways. The well-to-do citizens of the mansions in the Warmoesstraat and the Kalverstraat settled in the first section: Herengracht, Keizersgracht and Prinsengracht. The plots were laid out by Frans Hendriksz. Oetgens and Hendrick Jacobsz. Staets, on a mathematical basis rather than following the existing pattern of drainage ditches and pastures. This approach had already been applied to the Oostelijke Eilanden of Uilenburg, Rapenburg and Marken.

Amsterdam 1795

However, the straight radial roads connecting the canals provided only poor links to the city centre and the way in which the second area to be parcelled out, known as the Jordaan, was attached, was equally unsatisfactory. In the Jordaan, where small tradesmen and many Jews had settled, the division into lots did follow the existing pattern of ditches and pastures.

In dividing land into lots, space was reserved in both the Jordaan and within the belt of concentric canals for churches and public buildings which were not surrounded by large squares and parks. Neither public gardens nor wide prospects will be found in seventeenth century Amsterdam. The area to the west of the Amstel was quickly built up, whereas the eastern section lagged behind. Many Jewish immigrants settled here and rich Amsterdammers founded many charitable institutions. Between the concentric canals and the Oostelijke Eilanden, the Plantage was built, a promenade park with small country houses for well-to-do citizens. Now the Botanical Gardens are situated here.

The prosperity of Amsterdam was maintained throughout the

eighteenth century even though the port was surpassed in importance by London, Hamburg and Bremen. The rate of population growth decreased. The latest developments were sufficient to house all the inhabitants. Wealthy citizens built country houses along the Vecht and in the Watergraafsmeer which had been reclaimed in 1628. Only Frankendaal still reminds us of the former affluence.

The nineteenth century: a new start

In 1813 the French troops of Napoleon left the Kingdom of the Netherlands in a state of collapse. With the financial support and economic insight of King William I the Netherlands tried to revive the former glories of Amsterdam. In the first part of the nineteenth century improvements to the infrastructure laid the basis for economic development. This was only to gain momentum in the second part of the nineteenth century. The port was dredged and cut off from the Zuiderzee and reconnected with the sea in the north by the Noord-Hollandskanaal (1825). The opening of the Noordzeekanaal in 1876 and the Merwedekanaal in 1896 enabled Amsterdam to develop into an important port for transferring cargoes. The first railway, to Haarlem, was opened in 1839. Soon afterwards lines were laid to Utrecht (1843) and to Hilversum (1874), from the Weesperpoortstation. Not until 1889, the Centraal Station was built on an artificial island facing the waterfront on the axis of the Damrak to connect the lines from Utrecht to Haarlem.
The improved infrastructure stimulated industry. Shipbuilding flourished in the thirties and several factories were built on the outskirts of the town. The tram system and the gas and electricity companies were in private hands. This suited the more progressive liberals, who after 1865 had a great deal of influence in the city council.
The liberal council had to deal with the problems of a city that was very much impoverished, had a great number of unemployed people and an exodus of well-to-do citizens to dormitory towns in the Gooi and the Kennemerland. The poor and unemployed occupied vacant canal houses, converted them into smaller units and filled them from cellar to loft with their large families. Hygiene left much to be desired, especially because the canals were still used as sewers. Here too the liberals saw the solution in private enterprise, which considering the few powers left to the council under the constitution of 1848, was the only remaining possibility.
The land in the Plantage was released for building on by rich citizens. In 1838 the Natura Artis Magistra society had already built a zoo there. When in 1848 the city ramparts were demolished and a little later the city excises and tolls were abolished, expansion outside the ramparts became possible. The first expan-

Amsterdam 1866, with expansion plan Van Niftrik

sion included the areas on and along the city ramparts on which villas and other buildings were built. By setting up several businesses and by building the Paleis voor Volksvlijt on the Frederiksplein, Dr. Sarphati hoped to reduce unemployment, improve the city and raise the morale of its people. He was the first to propose a building plan for the working class as well as for the wealthy. In the area around the Frederiksplein only the buildings on the Westeinde, the Oosteinde and along the Hemonylaan, together with the majestic Amstel Hotel and the Sarphatistraat, which leads over the Hogesluis bridge, are left to remind us of his design.

The demand for houses increased in the rapidly industrializing town and many entrepreneurs followed Sarphati's example. Building activity began around the exit roads but quickly spread throughout the area up to the city boundaries. The city council realized that action was badly needed in order to preserve some vestige of cohesion. In 1866 the city architect Van Niftrik proposed an expansion plan, which, however, met with much criticism

12

Amsterdam 1877, with expansion plan Kalff

because the necessary, compulsory purchase of property did not conform to the liberal ideas of the city council. The plan consisted of a linked succession of working-class areas, villa parks and promenade parks. Many people see the influence of Haussman's plans for Paris in the geometrical street pattern.

In the final plan of 1876 by the director of Public Works Kalff and Van Niftrik only the Westerpark, the Sarphatipark and the Ooster-park are left to remind us of Van Niftrik's plan. The first two were carried out according to his designs. Apart from the Vondelpark (which was laid out privately), these parks were the only green spaces between the built-up areas. Kalff's plan took property boundaries into account and followed, as in the Jordaan, the alignment of pastures and drainage ditches. The city council assisted with the completion of the street network. This raised street rates and lowered building costs. Because Amsterdam, like so many European cities, made credit available, a real building revolution took place from 1874 till 1900, during which as many houses as possible were built on as little land as possible. The

development consisted of closed housing blocks around courtyards in which only the architectural treatment showed the
difference in social status between the different houses. Supervi-
sion of the building regulations was insufficient, so that many a
newly-built block of houses collapsed.

The council accepted responsibility for the infrastructure, but at
the end of the 1870's had the builders themselves pay for the
roads. Little consideration was paid to the way in which main
roads linked up with the old city as the junction of the Overtoom
with the Leidseplein shows. The irregular route of the Ceintuurbaan linked the main roads to each other and shows a lay-out that
was not very well planned. At the same time the arrival of office
blocks and department stores in the city centre made it necessary
to fill in many old canals such as the Spui, the Nieuwezijds
Voorburgwal and the Nieuwezijds Achterburgwal (now the Spuistraat) in order to create good connections to the Centraal Station.
The houses behind the Palace on the Dam had to be sacrificed for
the construction of the Raadhuisstraat. Traffic began to take its
toll.

Workers who could afford a new home settled predominantly in
the eastern and western parts of the nineteenth century belt, while
the better-off moved into houses along the Weteringschans, the
Plantage, the Sarphatistraat and, around 1900, the neighbourhood of the Museumplein.

Near the Kinkerstraat canals were dug partly to imitate the
character of the seventeenth century concentric canals, yet mainly
for reasons of hygiene. In addition to the improvement of
education and hygiene the housing of unskilled labourers became
part of the social question which after 1850 began to play an
important role in politics. However, the members of the philanthropical building associations were able to accomplish very little,
because they were unwilling to compromise the interests of firms
in which they themselves were the major shareholders. Their ideas
were to form the basis of the criticism of the Radical Liberals who
together with the Confessionals tried to defeat the Liberals. From
1890 onwards their influence was decisive. When in 1896 parts of
adjacent municipalities such as Nieuwer Amstel were annexed, the
land was leased out and observance of the building regulations
was more tightly controlled. Public transport as well as the
electricity and gas companies were taken over by the city council.
In addition to legislation to improve working conditions the
Housing Act was passed in 1901.

The council intervenes

Apart from a slight recession in 1923 the growth of the economy
and the increase in population continued until 1929. The Housing
Act of 1901 enabled the city authorities to draw up compulsory
building regulations and to grant subsidies to house builders,

Amsterdam 1915, with expansion plan Berlage

giving preference to housing corporations. Moreover, building materials had become too expensive for private individuals. Due to the increasing influence of the local authority in public housing, the Housing Department and Public Works became important institutions and became involved in the debate about town-planning theory. The districts around the Lairessestraat and the Willemsparkweg were built on land acquired by annexation. Work was started in the Indische Buurt, the Oosterpark area was completed and the Transvaal area, in which important architects such as Berlage were involved, was realized. The Transvaalbuurt amounted to a demonstration of the use of town squares. It is possible that some of Berlage's designs were preliminary exercises for one of the climaxes of pre-war town planning: the 1917 development plan for Zuid (Amsterdam South), see page 96.

This Plan Zuid was commissioned by the council to cover a section to the south of the Ceintuurbaan and was carried out in a somewhat revised form. It was the first time that aesthetic considerations had played an important role in planning. By combining wide avenues and winding side-streets, Berlage hoped to achieve the same mixture of the monumental and the picturesque which had characterized the seventeenth century concentric canals.

The avenues lead into squares in which monumental buildings were to have closed the perspective. Instead of artists' residences and an art academy, however, the buildings that were actually built were more mundane. A 'skyscraper' was built in the eastern part at the intersection of the Rooseveltlaan, the Vrijheidslaan and the Churchilllaan.

In the western part, dominated by a trident configuration of streets, a hotel was to appear at the end of the central axis.

Owing to the increased traffic, the squares have become busy traffic intersections. Seventy-five percent of all the buildings were intended to be working-class housing, making the plan an expression of the ideas, which were fundamental to the Housing Act. In Berlage's social vision all people were equal and, although the brief demanded a division into classes (the well-to-do came to live in the western part), Berlage was able to bring together the different classes by offering everybody the same environment.

The garden city concept, originating in England, was introduced to Amsterdam by socialist councillors such as Wibaut and De Miranda. These ideas were given shape in Tuindorp-Oostzaan, Volenwijk and with the incorporation into Amsterdam of the Watergraafsmeer in Betondorp.

The notion of garden suburbs was suggested by fears of megalopolis. In the opinion of architect Van Eesteren and town planner Van Lohuizen of the Town Planning Department, these fears were unfounded. In 1935 they produced the General Development Plan (Algemeen Uitbreidingsplan, AUP). This plan was unique in that it was based on a combination of requirements, resulting from statistical and demographic surveys. Housing, employment, transport and recreation were functions of a town, which deserved equal attention. The designers stated in the AUP of 1935, that Amsterdam would be complete in the year 2000 and would have around 900.000 inhabitants. Before the war, in 1934, a competition for cheap working-class houses was held as part of the AUP. It was won by representatives of the Nieuwe Bouwen (Functionalism). On the basis of their design, housing was built in Bos and Lommer, an area in the western part of the city. The closed block was abandoned in order to admit more sun and air and green areas became more important. The designers were not satisfied with the finished product, however, as the high price of land had compelled the builders to place the façades too closely together.

Slum-clearance in the Jordaan and the Oostelijke Eilanden, which had been started in the 1920's came to a standstill because of the Depression of 1929. Yet, in the thirties several railways were elevated and in 1939 the Weesperpoortstation was replaced by the more southerly Amstelstation. These actions were intended as part of a scheme for an orbital railway-line around the city. Together with the landscaping of the Amsterdamse Bos (landscape park) it was part of a job creation scheme.

After the second World War: expansion and renewal

When the war was over the city recovered surprisingly fast. After an initial increase the population now fluctuates around 700.000 but the AUP had not provided for the increase in car ownership and the demand for more living space per inhabitant. The Department of Housing and the Town Planning Department, responsible for most of the new developments, realized that the western suburbs of Geuzenveld, Slotervaart, Slotermeer, Osdorp, Westlandgracht and Buitenveldert in the south were inadequate. Building was also necessary in Amsterdam Noord and Amsterdam Zuid-Oost in the sixties.

Flats of more than five storeys appeared for the first time in the north of the city, which in 1952 was connected to the centre by the IJ-tunnel. The Coentunnel and the Schellingwouderbrug made completion of the ring-road round the city possible and protected Waterland, the polders north of the city, from further expansions. In the AUP the provision of landscaping received as much attention as housing, employment and transport. The Amsterdam-se Bos had already been laid out before the war and in the fifties suburbs in Amsterdam West were situated around the large Sloterplas (lake).

In the Bijlmermeer in Amsterdam Zuid-Oost the separation of different types of traffic according to function on different levels formed the structural theme. The area was connected to the centre by the metro. The Bijlmermeer, with its abundant greenery, separate traffic zones, large car parks and centrally situated shops, could have become the triumph of the ideas embodied in the AUP. Reference was also made to the ideas of CIAM. However, the large scale on which the Bijlmermeer was built, incurred much criticism and the district of Gaasperdam was laid out on a smaller scale with low-rise building.

The proximity of motorways and railway has made Zuid-Oost very attractive for the establishment of businesses. It is currently the biggest office building site in Europe. Apart from Schiphol airport these businesses provide most of the job opportunities. The resulting migration of firms from the town centre, is now a problem for the city council.

This development is the opposite of what was happening in the sixties. Then many businesses settled in the city centre and large roads threatened to devastate characteristic parts of the town. Of those large roads only the Wibautstraat was actually built. The construction of the metro, for which many houses were demolished in the Nieuwmarktbuurt (the former Lastage) met with much resistance from the local population. Their opposition led to a turning point in council policy with regard to urban renewal, on

which the population now has more influence. The Pentagon in Jodenbreestraat and housing around Nieuwmarkt are successful examples of this development.

Housing and employment in the city centre now receive equal attention, often owing to the neighbourhood action groups. Neighbourhoods eligible for urban renewal are renovated in phases, adhering to the nineteenth century infrastructure. The council now has the difficult task of keeping motor traffic out of the city centre without causing firms to think twice about establishing themselves there. Therefore, public transport is being improved and the use of bicycles stimulated. In 1978 the railway line to Schiphol from Amsterdam Rai (station) was opened and in 1986 the second Schiphol railway line, through the western part of the city, was brought into service. After fifty years, the orbital railway line will have been realised when Amsterdam-Rai station is connected to Duivendrecht station.

In 1985 two unusual plans were completed. For the IJ-plein Rem Koolhaas designed a plan in which urban villas and rows of low-rise buildings are placed in such a way that as many residents as possible have a view of the river IJ. Carel Weeber was responsible for the Venserpolder development, where, with reference to Berlage's Plan Zuid, he built closed housing blocks with large courtyards along wide streets.

Koolhaas' plan generally meets with approval, whereas the plan by Weeber arouses controversy. Both demonstrate that there is still a lively debate about town planning in Amsterdam. The council has plans to build offices, hotels, museums and houses along the river IJ and in the eastern docklands in order to stop the migration from the city centre. This has become a new proving-ground for town-planning ideas.

The compact city

During the 1970s the continued emphasis on urban renewal and social housing led to a large-scale exodus of the better off from Amsterdam. Because there was little opportunity for them to move up the housing ladder, they moved to rapidly growing neighbouring municipalities – initially with the encouragement of Amsterdam itself. Affordable single-family dwellings with gardens were available in these 'overflow municipalities', such as Almere and Purmerend. But the need for people to commute between these growth centres and Amsterdam each day caused enormous traffic problems. Furthermore, this exodus distorted Amsterdam's population structure. Amsterdam was compelled to respond, and policy shifted towards promoting the concept of a 'compact city'. Although with the construction of the Bijlmermeer the municipal-

Illustration p. 18/19
Algemeen uitbreidingsplan (AUP)

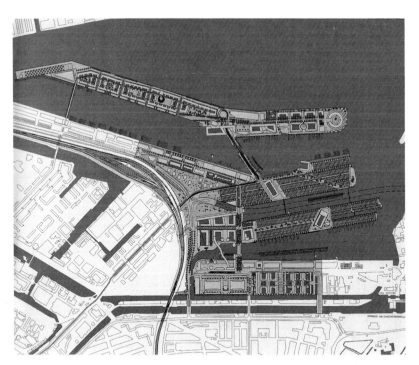

Oostelijk Havengebied

ity considered Amsterdam full, it went looking for new housing locations within the city's boundaries, preferring those that could also offer employment opportunities. By taking over sites abandoned by industry, urban enclaves have been created over the past few years which have their own unique atmosphere and style of architecture. The Oostelijk Havengebied, which is centrally situated in relation to the city centre, was rediscovered for example. And several hitherto undeveloped areas between the city's western suburbs were earmarked for housing. One example is the market-gardening district of Nieuw-Sloten. Under the terms of a 1988 covenant agreed with the state, a start had to be made on constructing 5767 dwellings in the Oostelijk Havengebied before 1996. The final target envisages the construction of 8500 dwellings housing around 17,000 inhabitants. A total of 33,000 dwellings will have to be built in Amsterdam over the next decade. The development of the Oostelijk Havengebied since the end of the 1980s demonstrates well how the emphasis of municipal policy and town-planning ideas have shifted. Though the earliest projects (along the Cruquiusweg) proposed constructing only social housing, on Java-eiland and Borneo-Sporenburg seventy per cent of all new housing will be for the free-market sector. Of particular interest though are the different architectural approaches taken by the projects.

The best-known project so far is KNSM-eiland, with the much discussed sculptural, brick housing block by the German architect Hans Kollhoff. For the island's remarkable location, in the middle of the IJ, the municipality opted largely for closed blocks in order to create a clear distinction between public and private. This reveals a completely different view from that taken a number of years previously in IJplein. The architect Jo Coenen was responsible for the detailed urban masterplan for KNSM-eiland.

In contrast, Sjoerd Soeters, who drew up the urban design plan for Java-eiland, rejected large freestanding blocks. He wanted the façades to be designed by different architects. In his plan four artificial canals transverse the long narrow island. What Soeters is particularly seeking here is the alternation of sight lines which results as one crosses a steep bridge. Furthermore, the combination of small canal houses and large apartment buildings creates differences of scale and atmosphere.

On Borneo-Sporenburg most houses will be single-family dwellings, with a density of around 100 dwellings per hectare. The firm of West 8 drew up the plan and developed a completely new type of dwelling, arranged around a patio, garden or roof terrace. The dwellings will be designed by various architects. Three large apartment buildings will 'rise up' between the streets of terraced houses. These serve to increase the dwelling density, but they also function as 'modern church towers', landmarks amid the low-rise.

Just as with Borneo-Sporenburg, the starting point in the district of Nieuw-Sloten was very high density low-rise. By stacking dwellings in the centre of the area, it was possible for most to be single-family dwellings. Here too, the high-rise served to provide a point of reference for the entire area. A clear structure and a carefully considered design of the public space have encouraged a further improvement in the quality of life in this densely populated area.

Following the Bijlmermeer fiasco, it was clear that good links and services are essential for the success of a new residential location. In this respect Nieuw-Sloten is very favourably situated – close to the ring road and Schiphol, but also close to existing services in surrounding areas. If the Oostelijk Havengebied is to be successful, good access will be essential here too. In the future, the peninsulas will be connected by transverse routes, and a car and high-speed tram link is to be built to connect the city centre to the ring road via the new Piet Heintunnel. A central shopping centre is to be built in the middle section.

Little came of the functional mix intended with this urban expansion. Over the past few years it has been around the World Trade Center (WTC) and in Amsterdam-Zuidoost rather than the new residential districts that significant concentrations of office space have appeared. Both the prestige offices around the WTC and the

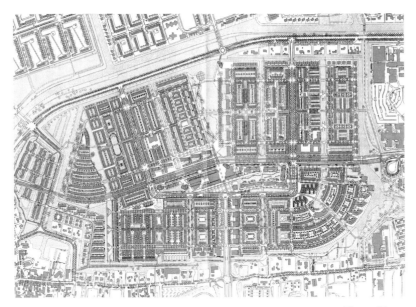

Nieuw-Sloten

ABN AMRO Bank's future headquarters are well situated as a result of their proximity to a railway and metro station. Furthermore, a north-south metro line is to be built at some stage to link the city to Amsterdam-Noord. A large office park has also been established close to Bijlmer Station in the past few years, in combination with a shopping centre for local inhabitants. The construction of the new Ajax Stadium is a major stimulus to the further development of the area. A wide shopping, café/restaurant and entertainments boulevard is to connect the areas either side of the railway line.

Grandiose plans for a wide IJ-boulevard along Amsterdam's waterfront – providing space for expensive offices, dwellings and cultural organizations – have been scrapped for the time being, although certain projects will be realized, such as the prestigious Science Centre in the Oosterdok.

In the future, Amsterdam will continue to expand, probably by building housing on a new artificial island in the IJ-meer. In order to meet the government's housing target, 18,000 dwellings will have to be built on this island, IJburg. Current plans include, among other things, dwellings *in* the water, which shows that, fuelled by new ideas, the intense debate on town planning is continuing to rage in Amsterdam.

Parks in Amsterdam

On a recent street map of Amsterdam one is immediately struck by two colours, green and blue. Blue represents the history of Amsterdam from when the city was founded on the spot where the rivers Amstel and IJ converge. The canals, waterways and lakes all have a history of their own. They are all from a later date, as are the cemeteries, public parks and gardens. Indeed, parks and gardens became common only during the course of the nineteenth century. Together with the roads, squares, façades and water, public green space has become the determining factor in the quality of public space in the city. Amsterdam's landscape depicts a unique situation.

Within the ring of canals

The planting illustrated on the well-known map by Cornelis Anthonisz. from 1544 is confined to a few vegetable gardens and orchards belonging to monasteries. Vegetables, fruits and herbs were grown there. The Begijnhof between Kalverstraat and Spui dates from 1346 but was later extended. Most of Amsterdam's *hofjes* were founded during the seventeenth and eighteenth centuries as almshouses. In 1610 plans were made to construct the famous ring of concentric canals, and the scheme was further elaborated in Daniël Stalpaert's map of 1665. A striking feature of this scheme was the canals lined with trees on both sides. As is evident from poems, travel stories, paintings and charters, great importance was attached to green space in the city's expansion. A *stadsgaardenier* (city gardener) was responsible for the trees in the city and for any new planting.

At that time, the authorities also regulated private gardens along the canals. On 19 November 1615 an ordinance was enacted which laid down conditions under which land was granted along parts of Herengracht and Keizersgracht. Local regulations permitted the owner of a plot to build on an area up to 100 *Amsterdamsche voeten*. (1 *voet* is 28 cm) from the street. In addition, a summerhouse was permitted at the end of the property as long as it was no more than 15 *voeten* deep. The space in between was left unbuilt and intended for a garden. The seventeenth-century architect Philips Vingboons designed a number of canal houses with adjoining geometrical gardens in which the same elements are present, namely vegetable gardens, *parterres de broderie* (embroidered parterres), bleaching grounds, summerhouses and aviaries. Even now, a number of luxuriant examples of this wealth of planting and of the sculptures and summerhouses exists.

From 1880 onwards the landscape architect L.A. Springer remodelled a number of canal gardens into country-house gardens according to the fashion of the time. From 1920 onwards J.R. Koning restored a number of properties (*keurblokken*) along the lines of seventeenth-century geometrical designs. The reconstructed gardens of the Museum Willet-Holthuysen and Huis van Loon, with its beautiful summerhouse, also have a markedly architectural structure.

Apart from having a canal house, wealthy owners often had an estate in the country or along the rivers Amstel or Vecht. By about 1700 there were about 400 such estates around Amsterdam, along the Amstel, the Haarlemmerweg, in Watergraafsmeer, in Kennemerland and in the Vecht region.

With the exception of Herengracht and Nieuwe Herengracht, the concentric ring of canals terminates at the Plantage in the east of the city. In 1682 the authorities decided to situate a pleasure garden between Nieuwe Herengracht, Plantage Muidergracht and Plantage Doklaan. This was the first sizeable green open space in Amsterdam. The architect J. Bosch divided the rectangular site into straight lanes along which privately owned gardens and places to relax were situated. The area became an important attraction and was, until 1940, a thriving entertainment centre. Even though part of the Plantage was built on in the nineteenth century, Artis (the zoo), founded in 1839 on the initiative of three individuals, continued to occupy most of the area.

Walking to the Plantage from the city via Plantage Middenlaan, one sees on the right the old Hortus Botanicus (the botanical gardens), established here in 1682, and, on the left, Wertheimpark, named in 1898 after the banker A.C. Wertheim. The park along Nieuwe Herengracht was laid out in 1812 by the civic architect A. van der Hart and was originally part of a larger site which included what is now a sports field behind the park.

Parks outside the ramparts

The gardens laid out on both sides of the Willemspoort in 1843 were enlarged two years later with a park on 't Blauwhoofd, a city fortification. This created a popular promenade to the river IJ, and offered the city's inhabitants a magnificent view towards the river Zaan and the Zuiderzee from near the present Houtmankade. Despite being extended in the direction of the Bogt (another fortification) in 1857, Park Blauwhoofd's existence was short-lived. The park disappeared in 1869 when a connecting canal was dug. These developments meant the city's outer limits had been breached however.

Park Blauwhoofd still featured in J.G. van Niftrik's famous 1866 expansion plan for Amsterdam. He planned a number of working-class neighbourhoods, urban-villa neighbourhoods and city parks in a new strip along Singelgracht. By 1855 responsibility for planting trees in the city was vested in the newly established Dienst van Publieke Werken (Public Works Department). Thus van Niftrik, as civic engineer, had considerable influence on both urban development as well as the layout of green open space.

Amsterdam's most famous park, Vondelpark, was a private initiative however. In its current state, little now remains of another private initiative, that by Samuel Sarphati, a doctor, who designed a luxurious, green residential district in Amsterdam's Oud-Zuid. The Sarphatipark (1885) is a vague memorial to Sarphati's intentions. Westerpark was probably designed by van Niftrik and laid out in 1891 on the site where, fifty years before, the first steam train left for Haarlem. This park and Oosterpark, which was completed in 1894 by the landscape architect L.A. Springer, were included in the urban-expansion plan drawn up in 1877 by the new director of the Public Works Department, J. Kalff. The smaller public gardens like Frederiksplein (1870) and Frederik Hendrikplantsoen (1883) outside the Singelgracht often included references to the planting at the former gates to the city. Some of the trees in the Leidsche Bosjes date from before the Leidsepoort was demolished in 1862.

Green space in large-scale urban development

At the beginning of the twentieth century Amsterdam had relatively little public green space in comparison with foreign cities. The fact was noted by a committee from the Amsterdamse Woningraad (Amsterdam Housing Board) and included in the *Rapport over de Amsterdamse Parken en Plantsoenen* (Report on the Parks and Public Gardens of Amsterdam). To improve the situation proposals were put forward by, among others, the architect H.P. Berlage and the conservationist J.P. Thijsse. Thijsse wanted to link the centre of Amsterdam with the polders outside the city by means of four green axes. Thijsse played a prominent role in setting up the Vereniging tot Behoud van Natuurmonumenten (Association for the Preservation of Nature Reserves). With the purchase in 1906 of Naardermeer near Amsterdam, the first nature reserve was established.

The need for green open space led local SDAP (Social Democratic Labour Party) councillors to provide the city's first playgrounds and allotments. In about 1915 the IJbos (later renamed after the socialist councillor W.H. Vliegen: Vliegenbos) and Volewijkspark were laid out in Amsterdam-Noord. The important routes in Berlage's *Plan Zuid* such as Apollolaan also show how, from the 1920s, the municipal authorities took seriously their responsibility for providing public space. Apollolaan has recently been renovated to a design by Bureau B + B. In 1926 a start was made on laying out the Zuiderzeepark (Flevopark) along the Nieuwe Diep.

The green connecting links propagated by Thijsse can be recognized in the Algemeen Uitbreidingsplan (1934), which included the 900-ha Amsterdamse Bos, and in the later struggle to preserve the green banks of the Amstel. In the case of major housing projects in and around Amsterdam, the Vaste Commissie voor Uitbreidingsplannen (Standing Committee on Extension Plans) gave detailed advice and paid considerable attention to the relationship between city and nature.

These new ideals also resulted in the provision of communal green spaces between blocks of houses. A good example of this is the communal garden designed by the landscape architect Mien Ruys at Geuzenhof, a 1930s public-housing project on Willem de Zwijgerlaan. The garden, which opened out onto the lower gallery of the block, included a stage for performing music and plays, an ornamental pool, an aviary and sandboxes. The garden was planted with simple indigenous plants. Ruys has designed many projects in Amsterdam which are worth a visit. They include communal gardens for housing in Frankendael (De Sitterstraat) (1949), which has a playground by Aldo van Eyck; the semipublic park at the Andreas Hospital (1967); and the small park at what used to be the offices of the KNSM (KNSM-laan, around 1950) and which she herself has recently adapted as part of the development of the Oostelijk Havengebied.

Most parks suffered considerably during the Second World War and profound renovations were necessary. This provided an opportunity to further elaborate the recreational function given to parks as an integral component in the design process by the Algemeen Uitbreidingsplan. The prominence of Sloterplas in the Westelijke Tuinsteden and of Gijsbrecht van Aemstelpark in Buitenveldert are indicative of a more intense interaction. Rembrandtpark (1973), plans for which had been drawn up even before the Second World War, links the older neighbourhood De Baarsjes, which dates from the period of the Amsterdam School, with the flats in the Overtoomse Veld.

In order to solve the problem of a lack of recreational facilities, in the 1960s the government resolved to lay out 'green stars', and larger areas close to the city were redesigned as places of recreation. It was as a result of this policy that Het Twiske to the north of Amsterdam and Spaarnwoude between Amsterdam, Velsen and Haarlem were developed. The high point of the green-city concept was reached in the 1960s when the Bijlmermeer was built. High-rise flats were built in a wooded landscape divided into so-called *woonhoven* (residential courts), local parks and large, green open spaces like Gaasperplas. The park at Gaasperplas was the result of the International Horticultural Exhibition, the Floriade, which was held in Amsterdam for the second time in 1982. In 1972 Amstelpark was laid out for the same purpose.

The most recent urban-development schemes of Nieuw-Sloten and the Oostelijk Havengebied, both of which are still under construction, illustrate a new vision in municipal policy towards green space. The landscape architect Lodewijk Baljon was supervisor for the architecture and public space in Nieuw-Sloten. In collaboration with the city's Dienst Ruimtelijke Ordening (Physical Planning Department), it was decided Nieuw-Sloten should be densely built but also retain an open character. The most significant features are wide sightlines across the lawns and the considerable attention paid to pavings and tree planting.

Those who conceived the layout of the Oostelijk Havengebied along the banks of the IJ started from the proposition that 'blue is green'. Following their design for a major extension to Schiphol, West 8 landscape architects designed an equally impressive green plan in 1992, one dominated by an enormous number of birch trees and clover.

Finally, the transformation of Museumplein into a park will be a dream come true for many. The design, by the Danish landscape architect Sven-Ingvar Andersson, envisages a meeting place in the midst of art.

Sloterplas

Frankendaal
c. 1660 5.3 ha

This seventeenth-century farmstead in the impoldered Water-graafsmeer was converted into a country estate during the eighteenth century. In 1835 it became a popular pleasure garden for the people of Amsterdam. Its attractions included a playground, a tearoom and an island with a hermitage set between poplar trees. In 1867 the Koninklijke Nederlandsche Tuinbouw Maatschappij 'Linnaeus' acquired Frankendaal and founded a nursery and a horticultural school. One of its students was L.A. Springer, who later became a famous landscape architect. The municipality of Amsterdam subsequently became the owner and established the city's nurseries here in 1886. H.C. Zwart, head of the city's parks department, and later, from 1923, J.R. Koning lived on the estate. In 1925 an open-air theatre was built in the woods behind the house, and two years later the first mass open-air lessons for children began. In the 1930s the school gardens and an allotment complex were added. The botanical garden was laid out by J. Jongsma in 1960. In 1982 this historic country estate became a public park. The Louis-XVI-style entrance gate is embellished at the front with Ionic pilasters, ferns and a medallion with the head of Mercury (Jacob Otten Husly, 1783). In 1951 the gate was modified again with the addition of the pinewood king-post originally from the Munttoren. Further restoration work followed in 1982. There is a fountain in a shell-shaped basin representing the sea-god Poseidon and his wife, the sea nymph Amphritite. In the middle, a small boy sitting on a dolphin plays the lyre (Ignatius van Logteren, 1714). See also **201**.

Old Hortus Botanicus
1682 1.7 ha

After the Plantage had been laid out on the edge of the old city, there was space over for the new Hortus Medicus. The plants and seeds supplied by the Dutch East India Company and the West India Company enabled an extraordinary collection of exotic plants to be built up. The semicircular hedges and the flower-beds are a reference to the seventeenth century. Later the Hortus was used as a research garden for the University of Amsterdam. The iron palm house on Plantage Kerklaan dates from 1912. A major renovation began in the late 1980s. The tropical hothouse, which consists of three separate glasshouses each with a different climate, was completed in 1993 to a design by Zwarts & Jansma and laid out by landscape architect Wybe Kuitert. A fine collection of old trees in Wertheimpark on the other side of Plantage Mid-denlaan recalls the period when the park was part of the Hortus.

Vondelpark

Vondelpark
J.D. Zocher & L.P. Zocher, 1864-65 8 ha
L.P. Zocher, 1877 40 ha

The park was laid out in the rustic area between Singelgracht and Amstelveenseweg on the initiative of the Amsterdam banker C.P. van Eeghen (1816-89). Up to 1953 Vondelpark was in private hands. The park was designed in two phases. The layout by Jan David Zocher jun. (1791-1870) and his son Louis Paul (1820-1915), both from a famous family of park designers, consists of meandering paths, pools and small groves alternating with open fields. The original plan envisaged exotic plants. During the past century the park has been repeatedly adapted to reflect the needs of the time. During the summer the park is crowded with tourists and people from the city. Vondelpark is to be the first public park in the Netherlands to be listed as a national monument. See **320** for the buildings and sculptures.

Zorgvlied
J.D. Zocher jun. & L.P. Zocher, 1867-69
L.P. Zocher, 1891-92
C.P. Broerse, 1967 14 ha

This cemetery is an enclave of the municipality of Amstelveen and lies along the banks of the river Amstel. The oldest part dates from 1867 and, like the extension in 1891-92, is laid out in the land-scape style. The most recent extension, by C.P. Broerse (1902-95), is laid out in a more rigid 'Roman' style. The monuments are situated amidst poplars, weeping willows and dark coniferous trees, which provide an appropriate mood. There are fine monu-ments to be seen, like the family tomb of Oscar Carré (1891, J.P.F. van Rossem and W.J. Vuyk, the architects of Circustheater Carré (1887)), and the last resting place of many famous Amster-dam personalities, such as the architect Eduard Cuypers (1927), sculptor Hildo Krop (1970), the painter Carel Willink (1983), and the charismatic entertainer and nightclub personality Manfred Langer (1994). See also **316**.

Sarphatipark
J.G. van Niftrik, 1881-86 4.5 ha

Little became of plans by Samuel Sarphati (1813-66) for a salu-brious residential district near Ceintuurbaan. In J. Kalff's extension plans for the city, only 4.5 ha (the equivalent of two building blocks in the urban grid) were devoted to creating a municipal park. The park has a meandering footpath linking the ponds, as well as typical landscape elements such as idyllic bridges and a small waterfall. On the other side of the park, which is at polder water level, water was pumped by what used to be a steam-driven pumping station (opposite the entrance to the park at the end of Eerste Jan van der Heijdenstraat) and drained off into the Boeren-wetering. The playground was a later addition. During the restoration of Sarphatipark in 1994 the paths were raised, the southern part was given a more wooded character and the north was re-planted with ornamental shrubs and perennials. For the Sarphati monument see **336**.

Nieuwe Oosterbegraafplaats
L.A. Springer, 1889-94 35 ha

From 1865 it was forbidden to bury the dead in churches or within built-up areas and so cemeteries moved to the outskirts of the city. The old Oosterbegraafplaats, laid out near what is now the Tropenmuseum in response to these regulations, later had to be cleared for the same reason. In 1894 the Nieuwe Oosterbegraaf-plaats was laid out along Kruislaan according to a design by L.A. Springer (1855-1940). His design utilized geometrical forms, but within an otherwise landscape style. There are the tombs here of poets, such as J. Perk and E.J. Potgieter, the writer Nescio (J.H.F. Grönloh), General J.B. van Heutsz, and a monument honouring those who fought in the resistance, with a sculpture by Hildo Krop (1948). Other cemeteries close to Amsterdam and worth vis-iting are the Portuguese Jewish cemetery Beth Haïm in Ouderkerk aan de Amstel and Huis te Vraag. Beth Haïm was set up in 1614 by two congregations of Amsterdam's Portuguese Jews: Beth Ja-cob ('House of Jacob') and Neweh Sjalom ('Place of Peace'). Huis te Vraag at Jaagpad near the Schinkel is now overgrown. It was laid out in 1891 as a private cemetery.

Oosterpark
L.A. Springer, 1891-94 12 ha

This square oasis was laid out along Linnaeusstraat in a working-class district of Amsterdam. Following a competition in 1891, Springer extended the park considerably behind the old Ooster-begraafplaats, where the present Tropenmuseum is located. As with the other nineteenth-century parks, the layout is based on an idealized landscape, but in this case with wide spacious foot-paths and fewer side-paths. The pond extends the entire length of the park and forms a partition between the old cemetery, which is situated higher, and the new park. The group of sculptures, the 'Titaantjes', is a reference to the novel of the same name by Nes-cio in which the characters hang around the entrance to Ooster-park night after night.

Flevopark
E.M. Mandersloot/J.R. Koning, 1932 23.5 ha

This park, which is situated between Zeeburgerdijk and Ooster-
ringdijk in Amsterdam-Oost, used to be called Zuiderzeepark or
Nieuwedieppark. A grass expanse extending some 14 ha was
laid out on a terrain whose level had been artificially raised with
soil excavated when the Coenhaven was dredged. The reed border of the Nieuwe Diep was included in the park. Since 1938 the
entrance to the park has been through the so-called Hekkepoortje
of the Muiderpoort. In 1813 the Cossacks entered Amsterdam
through this elegant grey stone gate and put an end to Napo-
leonic rule. In 1898 the gate was demolished as part of a scheme
to improve traffic access. It was kept in storage and later re-
erected at Flevopark. Flevopark and the Nieuwe Diep are popular
with water-sports enthusiasts. There is a swimming-pool, a ma-
rina and facilities for windsurfing too.

Amsterdamse Bos
Jacoba H. Mulder, 1931-37
Layout 1934-70 900 ha

In 1928 the municipality of Amsterdam decided to lay out a park
between the Nieuwe Meer, the ring canal of the Haarlemmer-
meerpolder and Amstelveenseweg. A Bos commission consisting
of a large number of experts on the natural environment, urban
development, recreation and landscape architecture was asked to
investigate how best to develop the park. On their advice, the land
along the shores of the older *veenplassen* of the Poel and the
Nieuwe Meer was preserved. Most of the extensive recreational
facilities were to be located in the middle of the park.
The park was to be planted along geographical lines with trees
indigenous to the forests of Western Europe. It was laid out as
part of the Algemeen Uitbreidingsplan according to a design by
the architects Cor van Eesteren (1897-1988) and Jacoba Mulder
(1900-88). Mulder was responsible for the design and execution
of the Bos plan, which provided for equal areas given over to for-
est, open space and water. A 300-km-long pipe-drainage system
formed the basis of the park, which in some places is 5.5 m below
sea level. From the hill, the highest point, there are fine sight lines
to the mostly landscaped layout, with its curved paths, ponds and
alternately open fields and thick forests.
All types of sport are represented. The separate paths for ramblers,
cyclists and horse riders are functional. There is also a hockey stadium, a camping site, and the Bosbaan, a wide canal used for boat
races. The farmhouse Meerzicht has been transformed into a restaurant and also houses the park museum. Between 1937 and
1945 P.L. Kramer designed about fifty wooden bridges for the
Amsterdamse Bos; they vary in shape and detail. The statue 'De

Amsterdamse Bos

Houten Kruiwagen' (The Wooden Barrow) by Leon van der Heijden was erected on the playing field in 1982 in honour of the 20,000 unemployed who had worked on this park since the 1930s as part of a relief-work project.

Beatrixpark
Jacoba H. Mulder, opened 1938 7 ha

This park on Diepenbrockstraat in Amsterdam-Zuid was initially planted with just perennials, pine trees and spruce trees. They were planted on the sandy soil deposited to increase the level of the park. A canal to the north-west which flows into a large pond made it unnecessary to fence off the park. Sitting on one of the benches on the four-meter-high flat-topped hill, one has a splendid view over the park. The year 1967 saw the construction of the children's pond, with its round stepping stones and fountains. It is surrounded on one side by a fine pergola and benches. During the Floriade of 1972 the park was adorned with demonstration borders, miniature gardens and a medicinal court. This court, with its unique collection of herbs, was laid out in the Renaissance style and consists of three sections separated by hedges of yew. A horticultural exhibition in the RAI's Amstelhal and a green border with a lily garden led to the new Amstelpark, which was laid out especially for the Floriade. In the face of moves to enlarge the RAI complex, the Vereniging Vrienden van het Beatrixpark, set up in 1982, managed to prevent the so-called Groene Zoom and the lily garden being destroyed. The park was recently improved and now includes the site between the Nicolaas Lyceum and the ring road.

Jac.P. Thijssepark
Design and layout C.P. Broerse, 1940-72 5.3 ha

To visit one of Amsterdam's finest parks one has to cross into Amstelveen. This neighbouring municipality is well known for the high quality of its green open space. The former head of the city's parks department C.P. Broerse made an important contribution to this. The Jac.P. Thijssepark, named after the founder of the Vereniging tot Behoud van Natuurmonumenten, is situated between Amsterdamseweg and the Amsterdamse Bos and was inspired by the traditional Dutch peat landscape. The mostly indigenous planting is grouped around smaller enclosed beds in which the traditional lawn is replaced by herbs. Other botanical parks in Amstelveen such as Braak, Mauritsplantsoen and Meander are also worth a visit.

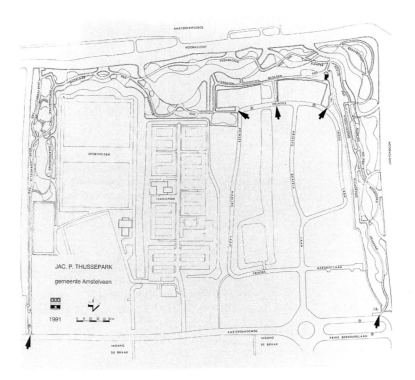

Gijsbrecht van Aemstelpark
Design and layout W.C.J. Boer, 1959-62 c. 40 ha

A narrow green strip in Buitenveldert links the Amsterdamse Bos with Amstelpark over a length of two kilometres. Wim Boer was one of the few landscape architects to join the *Opbouw* architects and the influence of that movement can be seen in his design. By continuing the pattern of the housing blocks in the geometrical design of the park, he produced an impressive integration of urban development and park architecture. The paths link up with the street layout of the area, and much use has been made of asphalt, concrete and stone. Near the shopping centre in the centre of the green strip is an island, intended as a place to meet. This square is enclosed by flower-beds, a pergola and a rectangular pond. A restaurant has been built on a peninsula to the east of the central square. A wide promenade lined with plane-trees runs parallel to Van Nijenrodeweg.

Erasmuspark
Egbert Mos, 1960-61 11 ha

There were gardens on this site even before the Second World War. Jan van Galenpark was situated here in the period after 1926. The present park to the north of Jan van Galenstraat in the Bos en Lommer district was completed only in the 1960s and after many plans had been drawn up. Admiralengracht broadens out along one side of the park and then flows into Erasmusgracht. Erasmuspark is laid out as a polder and has a geometrical structure enclosed by a dike to the north and the east. The water level in the park is the same as the polder water level, a few meters below NAP (the Dutch ordnance datum). The water in the surrounding canals is kept at the maximum level of the *boezem*, the polder outlets. The bridge across Admiralengracht along Jan van Galenstraat was built in 1933 to a design by Piet Kramer. The series of four sculptures by Hildo Krop (of an Eskimo with seals, an American stockbroker, a Negro with lions and a Chinese) represent the four points of the compass. Next to the steps and the incline leading to the path on the ring-dike around the park are two statues by J. Klaas (Mother and Child) and H. van Lith (Nude Standing).

Nieuwe Hortus Botanicus
C.P. Broerse, 1967 1 ha

This botanical garden was commissioned for a site along Van der Boechorststraat by the Free University of Amsterdam. It became an independent foundation in 1993. The hortus island, with its paths (a relic of the former scientific garden) along both sides of the main path, is now an ornamental garden. Of the young plant collections the bonsai and the rock garden are of particular interest. The complex of glasshouses is arranged geographically, and there are large collections of cactuses, succulents, carnivorous plants and orchids.

Het Twiske
Design 1968-90 M. Pemmelaar-Groot (supervisor
H. Schotanus and T. van Keulen/Grontmij)
Layout 1972-91 650 ha

Het Twiske lies to the north of Amsterdam, between Oostzaan, Landsmeer and Den Ilp. By extensive land-development work the architects have successfully restored the historic landscape within the ring-dyke, the remains of an unsuccessful attempt to impolder land. The pattern of land division is characteristic of the historic island area of Waterland. The layout of the park was largely based on the natural development of the land. On the other hand, there are facilities for cycling, hiking, sailing, horse riding, as well as passive recreation. Cars can be parked at one of the car parks on the edge of the park.

Spaarnwoude
Design Jacoba H. Mulder (municipality of Amsterdam), basic plan 1969 2750 ha

In 1965 plans were drawn up to lay out a recreation area in the polders surrounding the historic villages of Spaarnwoude and Spaarndam. Mulder's basic plan, completed in 1969, envisaged integrating nature, recreation and agriculture. The 2750-ha area, which lies between Amsterdam, Haarlem and Velsen, is divided into five smaller areas. The first is Houtrak near Halfweg (1971) and this was also designed by Mulder. The layout is closely related to that of her earlier design for the Amsterdamse Bos. South of the Noordzeekanaal and between the side channels B and C are Oosterbroek and Buitenhuizen. These were designed between 1975 and 1979 by G. Jol of the municipality of Velsen and they cover a total of around 385 ha. Buitenhuizen has a large public golf-course. Oosterbroek, in the north-west, borders on Buitenhuizen and can be recognized by the thirty-metre-high elongated hill. Some of agricultural land-lot divisions and their ditches have been preserved and given over to nature. With its combination of farmhouses and nature, Dijkland, another of these areas, forms an attractive peat land. The small lakes at Mooie Nel are suitable for water sports among other things.

Amstelpark
Egbert Mos, layout 1970-72 38 ha

In the design of this park too little advantage has been taken of the park's magnificent location along the Amstel. Nonetheless, this former Floriade site is one of the most attractive of Amsterdam's parks. The main entrance is on Europaboulevard to the east of Buitenveldert and a central, north-south pedestrian boulevard takes one through the park. To the left is Het Bastion, an elevated playground where children can ride ponies. From the 1972 International Agricultural and Horticultural Exhibition there remain several show gardens, such as a Rhododendron valley, the Dahliarama, a rose garden and an Italian arbour. The large botanical garden, the maze, the seals and the greenhouses are just a few of the attractions that make the park worth visiting. A special miniature Amstel train runs round the park. There is art too, in the form of a gallery and Het Glazen Huis. From the restaurant one has a beautiful view across the pond.

Amstelpark

Rembrandtpark
J. Theelen (D. Haan-Wiegman, supervisor municipality of Amsterdam), 1970-73 33 ha

The architect Cor van Eesteren had already envisaged a park on this site in the Algemeen Uitbreidingsplan (1934). It links the older residential areas of closed blocks with the high-rise at the start of the Westelijke Tuinsteden. Where the high-rise blocks begin, the park is transformed into roof gardens on half-sunken garages. The park is laid out in the landscape style, with slightly curved lines marked by ponds and paths. The Buiteltuin was presented to the city in 1970 by an Amsterdam department store. It is a new type of playground and was designed by artists from 'Group Ludic'. The climbing- frame construction is made from polyester.

The town garden of Museum Willet-Holthuysen
Design Egbert Mos, opened 1972 770 m²

Following a fire in 1929 Amstelstraat 20 and 22 lay fallow. The site had been obtained by the municipality of Amsterdam partly as the result of a legacy from the Willet-Holthuysen couple. A gift from a bank for the purpose of improving Rembrandtplein was used in part to lay out a garden behind the Museum Willet-Holt-huysen. This town garden was to be in the French classical style once popular in eighteenth-century Holland. It was laid out in 1972 by E. Mos, head of the city's parks department. Only a few plant types are used in this symmetrical garden. The central par-terres consist of clipped box hedges and red and white gravel. They are bordered by a grass verge. Pear trees and linden trees have been planted and these are trained against the trellises. As well as having an eighteenth-century sundial, the garden is em-bellished with a series of sculptures by Ignatius van Logteren dat-ing from 1721 and representing Flora, the goddess of flowers and spring, and Pomona, the goddess of fruit.

Gaasperpark
Design Pieter van Loon (supervisor J.W. van der Meeren), 1972-83 52 ha

Gaasperpark is at the point where the metro line to Amsterdam-Zuidoost terminates, between Bijlmermeer and Gaasperplas. It lies as a transitional green zone to the polders beyond. The main entrance with its straight lanes, which give way to a landscape with pollard willows along fields rich in herbs, the almost closed circles of hedges and the large ponds are the result of the Floriade held here in 1982. The exhibition had an instructive and educa-tional character. Wind energy was propagated as an alternative source of energy for glasshouse horticulture. And the provision of green space was central in, for example, presentations of graves and grave-side planting. Gaasperpark was rearranged fol-lowing the Floriade. It was reopened to the public in 1983 and with Gaasperplas forms a regional park extending some 140 ha. Some of the original Floriade elements, such as a perennials gar-den and a garden for heather, azaleas and grasses, have been pre-served. There are also sports and cultural facilities, as well as a playground.

French fruit garden in Watergraafsmeer
Jacques Vieille, 1994

In 1994, commissioned by the city of Amsterdam, the French artist Jacques Vieille designed a work of art close to the Gooise Knoop, the Gooiseweg exit from the ring road in Watergraafsmeer. The design consists of two elements. One is an assemblage of pylons. The second, a reference to Watergraafsmeer's lost pleasure gardens, is a 'fanned-out' fruit garden containing apple trees, pear trees and vines. The trees are trained along a series of screens placed in various directions and through which one can walk. The branches are pruned according to special patterns. The patterns are designed by students at the Florens College in Watergraafsmeer, and they are also responsible for maintaining the garden.

Museumplein
Design Sven-Ingvar Andersson, 1996-1998

Many plans have been drawn up over the past hundred years for this large triangular space behind the Rijksmuseum. In 1884 a garden was laid out around the museum according to a design by P.J.H. Cuypers, the Rijksmuseum's architect. It was designed in an eclectic style and functioned as a sort of outdoor museum, containing, among other things, fragments of old buildings, city gates and gates to country estates which had been removed from their original locations, statues, arbours and pollard trees. Despite the many designs for villas and parks, Museumplein has remained an open space. The idea of having a garden here continued to live on, however, and new plans were recently drawn up for the site. The 1993 design by the Danish architect Sven-Ingvar Andersson (pupil of C.Th. Sørensen) preserves the openness of the square, but the 1952 layout by the city's Public Works Department, with the 'shortest motorway in the Netherlands', will disappear, as will many of the trees. Instead, a pedestrian area with rivers, fountains, diagonally arranged rows of trees and flower-beds will be created. The proposed extensions to the Van Gogh and Stedelijk museums will be reduced to landscape elements in the park by a sloping expanse of grass. It is intended that the Concertgebouw will become a more prominent feature of Museumplein.

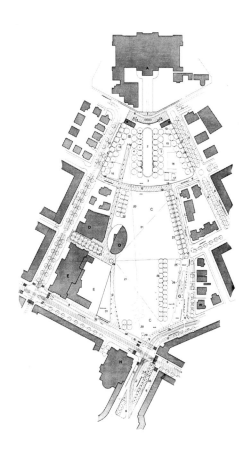

Before 1700

The first houses of Amsterdam were made of wood and consisted of three aisles. These houses were similar to the timber buildings still existing in Amsterdam Noord. Fairly early a more intensive land-use led to the adoption of a two-aisled type. At the end of the fourteenth and the beginning of the fifteenth century the one-aisled house that is so typical of the architecture of Amsterdam came into existence. Thus, the finished product was determined by local circumstances: narrow, deep and increasingly tall houses with steep roofs. The houses, built with timber frames and thatched roofs, had timber gables with each floor jutting out in order to throw rainwater clear of the façade. In the fifteenth century bricks increasingly took the place of timber. Owing to the risk of fire, a demand for safety measures arose. At first the timber side walls were replaced by brick ones, leaving the rest in timber. At the beginning of the sixteenth century the thatched roofs, which at first were coated with clay, were replaced by tiles. This was regulated by means of statutes (building regulations laid down by the city council). The timber gables too were gradually replaced by brick ones. In 1544 half of all the buildings still had timber gables. Two have survived up to now. The timber lower fronts were retained longest. In the middel of the seventeenth century Philips Vingboons was still designing buildings with lower fronts in timber. The earliest type of brick house was the house with a spout-gable, a literal translation of the timber house into the brick one, with projecting copings to throw water clear of the façade. An alternative to this was the simple step-gable.

Renaissance

The point of departure in the Renaissance is the building as an aesthetic unit derived from human proportions. Each part with its own dimensions and proportions, forms a harmonious unity with the building, and so a consistent system of proportions forms the basis of a renaissance building. To achieve this a thorough knowledge of the classical world of design was essential. In the second half of the sixteenth century pattern books by Serlio (1475-1545) for example, which were translated into Dutch, were relied upon in the Netherlands. In addition, pattern books by Dutchmen, such as Hans Vredeman-de Vries (1527-1606) which had much influence in the Netherlands, were published shortly

Nieuwendammerdijk
(Amsterdam Noord)
See map **100**

afterwards. His typical decoration was the strap and scroll ornament, derived from framing resembling incised and curled leather.

The typical step-gable, determined by the steep roof was a non-classical element that had to be absorbed into the ornamentation of the renaissance façade. The solution was an architecture with much emphasis on functional and constructively protective parts: in the relieving arches above wall openings, niche fillings, stringcourses in the brickwork and the gable endings with strap and scroll work, volutes, vases, escutcheons and masks. The space between the windows denoted pilasters, the space under the windows, whether or not in combination with stringcourses determined the entablature.

The culminating point of the Renaissance coincides with the period of architect Hendrick de Keyser (1565-1621) and his apparently decorative and playful façade architecture. The combination of the soft, red brick and yellow Bentheimer sandstone embellishment produces a clear and multicoloured imagery of construction and decoration: decoration constructively essential to protect the soft brickwork against the influence of rain. The renaissance step-gable architecture continues until the end of the seventeenth century.

Classicism

In the meantime a stricter conception of the use of classical elements was perceptible. Classicism began around 1625. Classical elements such as pilasters, entablatures and pediments were applied in such a manner that the façade was constructed in an apparently well-ordered manner. Again, Italian books of the orders, especially those by Scamozzi (1615), were used for this purpose. Pediments also made their appearance in architecture. The original function of the classical pediment is after all a covering and enclosing protection against rain and was, therefore, accepted as the means of capping gable ends and protecting windows. In the meantime the soft, red brick was replaced by a harder, brown brick. Through the use of pilasters, entablatures and pediments together with the introduction of a central emphasis by means of a central salient or pavilion, the step-gable changed, through the raised neck-gable (with rudimentary steps) into a neck-gable. At the same time a new decorative element appeared in the façade: the scroll. Where the raised neck-gable still had many fruit and flower ornaments, the neck-gable had many human and animal figures in the scrolls.

The larger and broader houses and the double houses began to resemble temple fronts: one or more tiers of pilasters with entablatures capped by a pediment and often decorated with garlands and festoons under the windows.

The most important architect of the first period was Jacob van

Campen (1595-1657), who built the Town Hall on the Dam. Later Philips Vingboons (1607-1678) and his brother Justus (1620-1698) appeared.

After 1665 austerity made its appearance: base, pilasters and festoons disappear. Instead, balconies and attics, sometimes sculptured, appeared. Emphasis was now on the harmony of parts and refinement of execution. The great architect of Restrained Dutch Classicism was Adriaan Dortsman (1625-1682).

Church-building

In the building of churches other influences played a role. For years Catholic churches had been built in the Gothic style with the altar as the dominant element. Even before the middle of the sixteenth century we see renaissance motifs and ornaments appear in the Gothic world of design. In the third quarter of the sixteenth century the breakthrough of the renaissance took place, as can be seen in the stained-glass windows and the purely classical architecture in the tower and the chapter house of the Oude Kerk. After the iconoclasm of 1566 the Alteratie took place in 1578, prohibiting the Catholic Church which took recourse in the building of schuilkerken (secret churches) in private houses. The Lutherans and religious groups other than the ruling Dutch Reformed were allowed to build churches, but without towers. The choir and the altar ceased to have a function in public worship and the pulpit became dominant. The renaissance ideal of central-ized building could now be put into practice. The Zuiderkerk was the first church in Amsterdam to be built for the Dutch Reformed community; a renaissance church, which follows the structural system of the Oude Kerk with timber trusses. As a result of the expansion of the city, the Westerkerk was built for the wealthy bourgeoisie who lived along the canals; on plan similar to the Zuiderkerk, but with a new structural concept. At the same time the Noorderkerk was built as a chapel for the poor who lived in the Jordaan. This truly centralised building was geared to a service in which the pulpit was dominant, whereas the structure is, again, traditional with timber trusses. Classicism continued with central-ized buildings as can be seen in the Oosterkerk and the Ronde Lutherse Kerk.

Oude Kerksplein 23
1300 onwards   Oude Kerk

The oldest part of this church, dedicated to St. Nicholas, is the tower which dates from 1300. In about 1505 several additions in the renaissance style were made by Joost Jansz. Bilhamer. From being a single-aisled church it developed, firstly, to a hall-church and, secondly, to a basilica. It has a rich interior with stained-glass windows of 1555 in the Mariakapel (Lady Chapel) by Dirk Crabeth and Lambert van Noort.

101   *centre* □

Nieuwezijds Voorburgwal 143/Dam
From the end of the 14th century –
Nieuwe Kerk

The result of a development beginning at the end of the 14th century, resulting in a late Gothic transept-basilica with ambulatory and radiating chapels. The church has timber and stone vaulting and an unfinished tower by Jacob van Campen. Inside can be seen the tomb of Michiel de Ruyter by Rombout Verhulst (1681), the copper choir screen rail by Lutma (1650) and the pulpit by Vinckenbrinck (1647).

102   *centre* □

Begijnhof 34
1460

Although the whole of the Begijnhof dates from roughly the same period, number 34 is the only one to retain its original timber gable. The timber structure of the house is also present in the other houses. They, however, have been provided with brick gables. The first floor was used for living and was reached by means of an external stair.

103   *centre* □

Prins Hendrikkade 94-95
1480 Schreierstoren

One of the defensive towers of the first city walls. The windows, doors and plaques are later additions. Characteristic is the round-arched frieze on which the battlements were formerly placed.

104 *centre* □

Nieuwmarkt 4
1488 St. Antoniespoort

The main building is flanked by heavy round towers. The city side has octagonal staircase towers. In 1545 it was altered by Alexander Pasqualini and Willem Dirksz. In 1617 it was converted to the Waag (Public Weighhouse). In 1691 it was used to house the dissecting room of the Guild of Surgeons. Note the brick bonding in the Bricklayers' Guildroom.

105 *centre* □

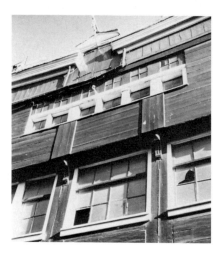

Zeedijk 1
c. 1550

This timber house has brick side-walls and a brick rear elevation, providing stability for the timber structure. The front façade has lost its original appearance (the lower front was replaced in the nineteenth century). However, it still gives a good impression of a medieval house. It is now part of a hotel complex.

106 *centre* ■

Oudezijds Voorburgwal 300
1550 Pakhuis Oudezijds Huiszittenmeesters

Two early examples of spout-gables. The original function of these warehouses was the storage of goods. In 1616 Hendrick de Keyser converted them into the pawnbroker's, which it still is. In 1669 it was extended with an austere, and for its time, modern building. The entrance gate with the city's coat of arms is somewhat in the style of Hendrick de Keyser.

107 *centre* □

St. Annenstraat 12
1565 Gulden Trip

This is the only small house surviving from the middle of the 16th century. The top is decorated with strap work and c-shaped volutes in the style of Hans Vredeman de Vries. The window frames are flush with the brickwork, which, unusually for Amsterdam, is executed in Flemish bond.

108 *centre* ■

Kalverstraat 92
Pieter de Keyser/Jacob van Campen/ and others.
1570 Burgerweeshuis

Orphanage with an entrance gate of 1581 by Joost Jansz. Bilhamer. The boys' courtyard dates from 1632. It has a loggia with 14 Doric columns, bearing shallow springstones and triglyph-consoles. The girls' courtyard of 1634 was executed in giant Ionic. Currently houses the Historical Museum (B. van Kasteel, 1975).

109 *centre* □

Singel 140-142
Hendrick de Keyser
1600   Vergulde Dolphijn

Lively façade owing to the mixture of stringcourses, springstones, keystones, masks, volutes and obelisks all in white sandstone and the hard, red brickwork. The façade of this building, in which Frans Banningh Cocq, commander of Rembrandt's *Nightwatch*, lived, is capped by two linked double step-gables.

110   *centre* ■

Zandstraat 17
Hendrick de Keyser
1603   Zuiderkerk

A pseudo-basilica six bays long, with Tuscan columns, timber barrel vaults and dormers. It has a richly, detailed tower, which can be seen clearly from the Groenburgwal: a square stone substructure, on which an octagonal sandstone section stands with freestanding columns on the corners. On top of this is a wooden, lead-dressed spire. Now an information centre for urban renewal.

111   *centre* □

Oudezijds Voorburgwal 14
1605   Burcht van Leiden

The upper storeys of this broad stepped gable with its simple stone decorations overhang the lower storey. The frieze above the wooden lower front of the building has the lion's masks, to which the building owes its other name of Leeuwenburg, and a stone tablet with the coat of arms of the city of Riga, the client's original home.

112   *centre* □

Nieuwmarkt 20-22
1605

The stone details all project from the brickwork, causing a play of shadows over the façade of this double step-gabled house. The fine 17th century-looking lower fronts of the building are not original; they had cross-windows, similar to the first floor, with the entrance in the middle.

113 *centre* □

Oude Hoogstraat 24
Hendrick de Keyser (attrib.)
1605   Oostindisch Huis

The richly detailed entrance is constructed from cushion blocks and has a round window over a door surrounded by volutes. It is flanked by cross-windows, above which the tympani have volutes and masks. The crown is a rarity: an ensemble of volutes, scrolls, stone-dressed window openings and a balustrade.

114 *centre* □

Singel 423
Hendrick de Keyser
1606   Bus- of Tuighuis

Richly decorated trapezium-shaped gable with volutes, triglyph pilasters, lion's masks, scrolls and a straight cornice with orbs. A modern façade for its time owing to the lack of stringcourses. It was used as a store for gunpowder and arms. Nowadays part of the University of Amsterdam Library.

115 *centre* □

Oude Waal/Oude Schans 2
Hendrick de Keyser
1606   Montelbaanstoren

The lowest part dates from 1512 and was part of the defences along the Oude Schans. On this Hendrick de Keyser built an octagonal section and a lead-dressed open-work timber steeple (also called Mallejan), which much resembles the tower of the Oude Kerk. Nowadays the offices of the City Water Authority.

116 *centre* ■

Oudezijds Voorburgwal 22
Hendrick de Keyser (attrib.)
Early 17th century – Int Slodt Egmondt

In this façade, cartouches link twin pilasters on which are set stone accolade arches and masks. On the finely carved beam over the timber lower front rests a frieze with two lion's masks and a stone tablet depicting Egmond Castle. The top section of the façade is of a later date.

117 *centre* ■

Oudezijds Voorburgwal 249/Grimburgwal/Oudezijds Achterburgwal
Claes Adriaensz.
1610   Huis op de drie Grachten

The front façade has a strong horizontal articulation caused by the sandstone strips. The cross-windows are placed in semicircular niches. All three façades are closed by a simple stepped gable. In the restoration of 1910 elements which had been lost in previous alterations were restored.

118 *centre* □

Waterlooplein 211/213-219
Willem de Keyser
1654/1610 Huiszittenaalmoezeniers-
huis en Stadsturfhuizen

211 – This simple façade has a central pavilion with cornice (brickwork frieze) and pediment. The governors' room with fireplace and decoration scheme are still present. Currently houses the Academie van Bouwkunst (Architectural Academy).
213-219 – Two spout-gables and a trapezium-shaped gable with balustrade. Horizontal emphasis given by stone stringcourses, vertical emphasis by means of the openings. Houses the Architectural Centre Amsterdam (AR-CAM).

119 *centre* □

Koestraat 20
Hendrick Gerritsz.
1611 Vergulde Leeuwshooft

The oldest known neck-gables, in which the stone scrolls call to mind the scroll-like infill of stepped gables. In 1633 it served as the wine-merchants' guildhouse. A statue of their patron saint, St. Urbanus, stands in the broken pediment of the entrance gate, designed by Pieter de Keyser.

120 *centre* ■

Kattegat 4/6
1614 Gouden en Zilveren Spiegel

Two simple stepped gables with pilasters at the summit. The cross-windows are placed flush with the façade and have arches with springstones and keystones which are made from the same yellow bricks as make up the horizontal bands in the façade, rather than from the usual sandstone.

121 *centre* □

Herengracht 120
1615 Coningh van Denemarken

This façade is almost in its original state, with a central entrance which was decorated at a later date. Functional stringcourses take advantage of the shape of the stepped gable with its volute scrolls. The balustrade on the second floor suggests a greater façade width.

122 *centre* ■

Haarlemmerstraat 75
1615 Kleine Vleeshal/
Westindisch Huis

Only the elevations of the courtyard retain their 17th century appearance. In 1623 the building was rented to the West Indische Compagnie, to which it owes its present name. In 1647 the Nieuwezijds Herenlogement was established here. It was rebuilt to house the Lutheran Orphanage in 1826. It has recently been restored and is now used for weddings.

123 *centre* □

Oudezijds Voorburgwal 57
Hendrick de Keyser
1615 Gecroonde Raep

Stepped gable divided horizontally by cornices, which serve as stringcourses. The double pilasters which form the window piers are linked by escutcheons. Above the windows are masks set between convex and concave volutes; below the windows are busts surrounded by volutes, resulting in an extremely decorative façade.

124 *centre* ■

Herengracht 170-172
Hendrick de Keyser
1617   Huis Bartolotti

This large, rich house stands on a bend in the canal, which is expressed in the façade. The top part of the façade is a stepped gable with stringcourses which are interrupted here and there, balustrades and tapered pilasters. Note the triglyph decoration which has piping instead of the usual grooves. Part of the building is now occupied by the Theatre Museum.

125   *centre* □

Nieuwebrugsteeg 13/St. Olofspoort
1618   In de Lompen

Renaissance stepped gable in the manner of Lieven de Key. The façade is subdivided by stone bands which correspond to the sills of the cross-windows. The frames are set in semicircular arched niches whose keystones are carved with heads of humans and lions. A good example of an early 17th century shop with dwelling above.

126   *centre* □

Muntplein
Hendrick de Keyser
1619   Munttoren

Originally formed part of the Regulierspoort of 1490. The brick base is partly round and partly polygonal and becomes octagonal higher up. Above this are four aediculae with segmental pediments on which the clockfaces rest. The octagonal lantern is entirely of timber dressed with lead and with an openwork orb. Coins were minted here in 1672 and 1673.

127   *centre* ■

Nieuwezijds Kolk
1620   Korenmetershuisje

There was already a corn measurers' house here in 1558. In 1620 it was replaced by a simple, rectangular building with basement, main floor and roof. Elevations with niches containing cross-windows. On the south side above the entrance is a stone tablet depicting the corn measurers' attributes. Now the offices of the Bond Heemschut.

128   *centre* □

Noordermarkt 44-48
Hendrick de Keyser
1620   Noorderkerk

Hendrick de Keyser's last church. It had a modern plan for its time: a Greek cross with small triangular additions between its arms. The façades are very simple and austere and are slightly reminiscent of neck-gables. Because they are lower than the ridge of the main church the four gables have been given hipped roofs.

129   *centre* ■

Prinsengracht 279
Hendrick de Keyser
1620   Westerkerk

A fine renaissance church which is a development of the earlier Zuiderkerk. The 85 metres high spire is made up of decreasing cubelike sections and is topped by the imperial crown from the Amsterdam coat of arms. There is still a gateway to the churchyard adjoining the tower. Rembrandt's grave is situated in the interior.

130   *centre* □

Keizersgracht 123
Pieter de Keyser
1622   Huis met de Hoofden

One of the largest double houses of the
period. The piers between the windows are wide Doric pilasters (with
carvings of, from left to right, Apollo,
Ceres, Mars, Pallas Athene, Bacchus
and Diana) which are extended upwards as double pilasters. Stepped gable with balustrades, niches and a
curved pediment. Now houses the
offices of the Gemeentelijk Bureau
Monumentenzorg (Council for the
protection of Historic Buildings).

131   *centre* ☐

Keizersgracht 177
Jacob van Campen
1624   Coymanshuizen

Double house with a façade in the style
of Palladio and Scamozzi, with pilasters and heavy cornices. At the lower
level the pilasters are Ionic and above
Composite. Note the absence of per-
rons, gable-end, balustrading and
playful decoration, resulting in a taut,
austere elevation.

132   *centre* ■

Nieuwendijk 30
1630

The vertical emphasis in this stepped
gable is reinforced by the continuous
niche which runs from the second floor
to the round attic window. The two
small windows in niches on each side
of the attic window are elements
which were to be used 15 years later in
the classical pilaster façade. Now part
of a hotel complex.

133   *centre* ■

Singel 411/Spui
Pieter de Keyser (attrib.)
1633   Oude Lutherse Kerk

Appears from the outside to be a two-aisled church on an irregular site; on the inside a rectangular hall church. On three sides there are two tiers of galleries. The church has been repeatedly altered and restored. Now in use as the assembly hall of the University of Amsterdam.

134   *centre* □

Jodenbreestraat 4-6
Jacob van Campen
1633

1606 stepped gable changed in accordance with Scamozzi's book of orders. It was the first house in Amsterdam to be capped by a pediment. From 1639 to 1658 the house was occupied by Rembrandt and it now houses the Rembrandthuis Museum. Interiors by K.P.C. de Bazel.

135   *centre* □

Nieuwezijds Voorburgwal 75
1633   Makelaarscomptoir

Asymmetrical façade caused by the pointed site resulting from the traditional street pattern. Cross-windows with continuous stone bands, springstones, keystones and volutes. On the last step is a niche with a shell motif above which is a triangular pediment. Still used as a 'guildhouse' by brokers.

136   *centre* ■

Sloterkade 21
1634   Aalsmeerder Veerhuis or
           Bonte Os

This formerly isolated building consists of a hall, corresponding to the width of the wooden entrance front, with a stepped gable. Adjoining this are side rooms which are two window bays wide. Various organisations involved in restoration work are now accommodated here.

137   *tram 1, 6* □

Brouwersgracht 188-194
1636   Koning David, David,
           Groene & Grauwe Valk

Four warehouses with fine, simple spout-gables front and rear. The linked hatches in the middle are now glazed. The two adjacent windows also had shutters originally. They were good examples of 17th century functional building and have now been converted into apartments.

138   *centre* ■

Kromboomssloot 18-20
1636   Schottenburg

Fine example of warehouses from the first half of the 17th century. The linking of the two warehouses gives rise to asymmetrical gable ends. Simple window-frames in niches with brick arches. The hatches are linked vertically. Now converted into apartments.

139   *centre* ■

Oudebrugsteeg 7/Beursstraat
Jacob van Campen (attrib.)
1638   Accijnshuis

A classical building with giant pilasters set on pedestals. The Ionic capitals support a straight cornice and attic to which windows were added at a later date. The old and new city coats of arms can be seen in the façade (Koggeschip and the three crosses).

140   *centre* □

Herengracht 168
Philips Vingboons
1638   Witte Huis

Entire façade in white sandstone with a step as a gable ending with extremely austere scrolls and vases. The client, Michel Pauw, Knight of St. Mark, had the two lions of St. Mark placed at the top as shield-bearers. Fine 18th century interiors by Jacob de Wit and J. de Moucheron. Now used as a theatre museum.

141   *centre* □

Keizersgracht 319
Philips Vingboons
1639

First example of Vingboons' use of pilasters in the façade of a narrow house. The two pairs of Doric pilasters support triangular pediments above the second floor. The top is decorated with pediments, scrolls, garlands, vases and two oval windows set in a waterleaf decoration.

142   *centre* ■

Staalstraat 7ab
Pieter de Keyser
1641 Saaihal

A trapezoid gable with draped sheets
which are also entwined around the
corner vases. The Amsterdam coat of
arms is set in a cartouche above the
tablet bearing the date. The façade of
this Drapers Hall is topped by the
imperial crown. The cross-windows of
the first floor have triangular pediments.

143 *centre* ■

's Gravenhekje 1/Prins Hendrikkade
Pieter de Keyser (attrib.)
1642

These four warehouses are united by
the two trapezium-shaped gables.
These gables, which are pierced by
oval and round attic windows, are in
turn linked by a pediment decorated
with festoons and a coat of arms bearing the monogram of the West Indische Compagnie.

144 *centre* ■

Bloemgracht 87-89-91
1642

A good example of traditional 'burgh-
er' architecture. Three stepped gables
built on a minimal frontage with timber
lower fronts, cross-windows in niches
with elliptical arches and tablets representing the 'townsman', the 'country-
man' and the 'seaman'. The stepped
gables are capped by corbelled pinnacles.

145 *centre* ■

Oude Turfmarkt 145
Philips Vingboons
1642   House of P.J. Sweelinck

A pilaster façade with three tiers of pilasters: the Tuscan, Ionic and Doric orders on a rusticated base. The façade of this building, originally one half of a twin property, is given an extra vertical emphasis by the recessing of the cornice in the middle bay. The rear part of the building is still intact. The building is now part of the university complex.

146   *centre* ■

Dam
Jacob van Campen
1648   Stadhuis van Amsterdam

Sometimes called the eighth wonder of the world. A large building built around two courtyards between which is the grand hall. On a base two orders of pilasters support minutely carved cornices. The central pavilions have pediments with allegorical carvings by Quellien, who was also responsible for much of the interior sculpture. The town hall is now used as a Royal Palace.

147   *centre* □

Palmgracht 28-38
1648   Rapenhofje

Almshouses founded by Pieter Adriaensz. Raep for elderly women and orphans belonging to the Reformed Church. On the street side it is a modest building with an entrance gate, a coat of arms and a barred cross-window. Entrance by a simple door which can be opened fully or partly. Around the courtyard is a row of houses which still have their original cross-windows.

148   *centre* □

Karthuizerstraat 21-127
Daniel Stalpaert
1650   Nieuwezijds Huiszitten-
        weduwenhof

This complex consists of the earliest
type of dwelling: the one-roomed
house. The simple façade has a central
pavilion with pediment and two side-
pavilions. The gutter board forms a low
cornice. The striking lintels above the
windows are in carefully rubbed red
bricks. In the courtyard the pediments
display the Amsterdam coat of arms.

149   *centre* □

Singel 83-85
1652   Veerhuis De Zwaan

The front and side elevations, which
both lean forward, have pilasters with
Ionic capitals bearing a continuous
cornice. Under the windows are festoons and date plaques. The lowest
festoon of the middle bay has a hanging cloth rather than fruit.

150   *centre* □

Oudezijds Voorburgwal 316
Philips Vingboons
1655   Ladder Jacobs

The central element with its Doric and
Ionic pilasters supports a straight cornice and a pediment with an 'oeil-de-
boeuf', festoons and swags. On the
second floor the fruit festoons become
swags at the supports. The stone tablet
shows a pilgrim at rest and two an-
gels.

151   *centre* ■

Kattenburgerplein 1
Daniel Stalpaert
1655 's Lands zeemagazijn

A sturdy, square storehouse with projecting pavilions in the middle and on the sides. One of the pediments, all of which were designed by Quellien, represents the Admiralty with sea deities and cannon. Another depicts Neptune and Amphitrite. Now houses the Scheepvaart Museum (Navigation Museum).

152 *centre* □

Keizersgracht 214
1656

A pilaster façade with giant Ionic order on the first and second storeys and entablatures in the outer bays only. The attic floor has a raised neck-gable with Corinthian pilasters and round windows with moulded surrounds. Built in the style of Philips Vingboons.

153 *centre* ■

Zandhoek 2-7
Second half of the 17th century

A terrace of quaint, modest houses from the second half of the 17th century. They all have a high lower front concealing two storeys. The remaining storeys are more obviously expressed.

154 *centre* ■

Herengracht 364-370
Philips Vingboons
1662   Cromhouthuizen

Four façades entirely in sandstone, built for Jacob Cromhout. Each has a central element, festoons, window pediments and oeil-de-boeufs. The first two buildings are clearly wider than the last two. Nr. 366, in which the Bible Museum is now located, has interiors by Jacob de Wit.

155   *centre* □

Singel 460
Philips Vingboons
1662   Odeon

Built on the site of the former brewery 'Het Lam' as a residence for the merchant Marselius. It has a raised neckgable and festoons under the windows. The scrolls have been given pinnacles. A cartouche surrounds the hoisting-beam. One of the rooms at the back of the building has a fine 19th century interior **(304)**.

156   *centre* □

Kloveniersburgwal 29
Justus Vingboons
1662   Trippenhuis

The composition is determined by eight giant Corinthian pilasters. The central pavilion supports the pediment which was richly decorated by Jan Gijselingh de Oude. The second and sixth bays, in which the entrances are situated, are wider and more richly decorated. The frieze is decorated with putti and arabesques. Note the chimneys made to look like cannons – the client was an arms merchant.

157   *centre* ■

Oudezijds Voorburgwal 40
1663   Schuilkerk Het Haentje

Simple but well-proportioned spout-gable standing on a timber lower front. The secret church, also known as 'Onze Lieve Heer op Zolder' and dedicated to St. Nicolaas, is on the top floor. The mid-18th century altar depicts the baptism of Christ. Now Museum Amstelkring.

158   *centre* □

Oudezijds Voorburgwal 187
1663

This merchant's house has a raised neck-gable with Corinthian pilasters and scrolls with carvings of Africans and Indians, reclining on bales of tobacco. As is often the case, this raised neck-gable has circular windows set in cartouches. The middle element with Ionic pilasters has fine festoons.

159   *centre* ■

Singel 11/Kattegat 2
Adriaan Dortsman
1668-1671   Ronde Lutherse Kerk

This round, domed church which has an ambulatory on half its circumference was burnt to the ground in 1822 in a fire caused by careless plumbers. Rebuilt in 1823 by T.F. Suys and J. de Greef, who gave it a coffered vault instead of the smooth vault with ribs.

160   *centre* □

Wittenburgergracht 25
Daniel Stalpaert
1669   Oosterkerk

Plan in the shape of a Greek cross in which the space between the arms has been partially filled by lower volumes. On the canal side is the main entrance whose elevation has a balustrade. The cornice of the lower volumes follows the relief of the walls whereas the cornice of the Greek cross strictly follows the plan without acknowledging the indentations of the wall.

161   *centre* □

3e Weteringdwarsstraat 33
Philips Vingboons
1670   Wevershuisje

One of the four hundred weavers' houses built for the city of Amsterdam. The 'voorhuis' has a timber entrance front with a simple staircase. Large, simple windows determine the elevation which is closed by a low cornice serving as a gutter. A good example of social housing in the 17th century.

162   *centre* ■

Nieuwe Amstelstraat 1-3
Elias Bouman
1670   Hoog Duitse Synagoge

This synagogue has austere elevations which are closed by a low cornice. The tripartite division of the elevations is achieved by the pilasters. The central part of the front elevation has a simple pediment on a slightly projecting cornice. Converted into Joods Historisch Museum (Jewish Historical Museum), by A. Cahen/Premsela Vonk, 1987.

163   *centre* □

Amstel 216
Adriaan Dortsman
1671   Gijsbert Dommer Huis

A flat façade with strongly banded stone window piers. Above the entrance is a balcony with a simple window surround. Above the frieze with its triglyphs is an attic in the form of a balustrade with its central part hollowed out to accommodate the leaf-shaped coat of arms.

164 *centre* ■

Keizersgracht 672-674
Adriaan Dortsman
1671   Museum Van Loon

Flat, stone elevations with single pilasters on the corners. The entrance is emphasized by the balcony and a concave section of the blind balustrade. The façade is closed by a triglyph-frieze above which is a partly open and partly blind balustrade with the characteristic 'bottle-shaped' balusters. There are statues on the balustrade.

165 *centre* □

St. Antonies Breestraat 69
Elias Bouman
1671   Pintohuis

The façade is given a strong vertical emphasis by the superimposition of the buttresses on the wall piers. The cornice, which echoes each indentation in the façade, carries a blind balustrade to conceal the roof. Now houses several organizations concerned with the preservation of historic buildings.

166 *centre* □

Oudezijds Achterburgwal 201/Rusland
1673

A slender raised neck-gable divided by pilasters. The two outermost pilasters have Ionic capitals and the two innermost have Corinthian capitals which bear a segmental pediment decorated with a shell motif. The stone tablet depicts a cooper.

167 *centre* ■

Mr. Visserplein 1-3
Elias Bouman
1675   Portugees Israëlitische
           Synagoge

The low buildings around the synagogue enclose a courtyard. The front elevation is subdivided by pilasters, the ones at the corners standing slightly free of the corner itself. The austere elevations with the corner bays slightly recessed are closed by a cornice above which is a balustrade and attic.

168 *centre* ■

Herengracht 394/Leidsegracht
Last quarter of the 17th century –
Vier Heemskinderen

This little house has a neck-gable with a segmental pediment. Fine façade tablet depicting 'the four Heemskinderen' on their horse Beyaart (characters from a medieval legend). There are simple festoons under the windows and around the hoisting beam.

169 *centre* ■

Amstel 51
Hans Petersom
1681-1683   Diaconie Oude Mannen-
                  en Vrouwenhuis

With its 31 bays this was the widest building in the city. The main entrance with Ionic pilasters is situated in the middle five bays which carry a simple pediment. The two side entrances have Doric pilasters. The austere character of the elevational treatment can best be seen in the façades of the inner courtyard.

170   *centre* ■

Prinsengracht 857-897
Pieter Adolfse de Zeeuw
1695   Deutzenhofje

These almshouses were for destitute women of the Reformed faith. The entrance has simple stone pilasters and an almost 18th century cornice with two putti. A stone tablet records the foundation date. The trustees' room above the entrance is decorated with festoons and the family coats of arms of the clients.

171   *centre* ■

Kloveniersburgwal 26
1696   Klein Trippenhuis

This small sandstone façade is only one bay wide (2.5 metres). The low cornice, which is raised in the centre to a semi-circle, carries two sphinxes. The frieze has festoons and an hour glass.

172   *centre* ■

Eighteenth century

The seventeenth century was a period in which architecture, like the economy, was thriving. During the eighteenth century prosperity was maintained, but the gap widened between the rich and the poor. The population as a whole hardly increased. There was, therefore, little demand for new housing development.

Nevertheless, building activity did not altogether cease. Many older, often seventeenth century, houses were rebuilt. They were provided with a new façade or even an entirely different interior. Most of the canal houses dated as eighteenth century have, in fact, a similar older core.

The country houses of rich Amsterdammers are often conversions of older property. Only Frankendaal still remains of the numerous estates in the Watergraafsmeer. Along the Amstel, Amstelrust and Oostermeer are still in existence.

This period of greater poverty among the people created the need for better services for the poor. Several new 'hofjes' (almshouses) were founded, of which Corvershof and the Van Brants-Rushofje are the most important from the architectural point of view.

The Louis Styles

Around 1700 the Amsterdam street scene was very varied on account of the great variety of gable types. For the rest of the eighteenth century too, gable endings, such as the neck-gable and bell-gable, remained common for the smaller private house. These gables are suitable for concealing the roof, which is at a right angle to the street. The eighteenth century neck-gables and bell-gables are often higher than those of the century before. The decorated stone scrolls are embellished in the various Louis styles, which, in imitation of France, became fashionable in the course of the century.

In the first part of the century, the Louis XIV style with its somewhat heavy, baroque shapes was adopted especially on the neck-gables. The often asymmetrical rococo shapes of the Louis XV style, which was used in the third quarter of the century, were not very suitable for the rectangular neck-gable. The bell-gable was now preferred. The strong and regular Louis XVI style of about 1780 was not often seen in conjunction with gable ends. Prinsenstraat 12 is the only neck-gable of that period. Numerous simpler types existed alongside the richly worked neck-gables and bell-gables. The neck-gable was marketed as an 'of-the-peg' article, which sometimes caused problems with adaptation to the plot width. This then led to the addition of, for example, vases on the corners.

The straight cornice was considered more suitable for wider houses with more than three bays and in which the ridge of the roof was parallel to the street. Many seventeenth century houses were provided with such a cornice and attic during the eighteenth century. Herengracht 476 is a fine example of this. In the seventeenth century the cornice served mainly as a gutter for the drainage of rainwater. In the course of the eighteenth century it was also given a clear architectural significance. The cornice, applied with great freedom and refinement, together with an attic often formed the crowning glory of the façade. The attic was often entirely or partly worked open as a balustrade, above which statues and other ornaments were sometimes placed. These decorations were similar to the gable ends in the different Louis styles. The Regency style, which developed as a transitional form between the Louis XIV and Louis XV styles in France, was only followed to a slight extent in Amsterdam around 1725. Huize van Brienen at Herengracht 284 is an exceptional example of this. If a straight cornice instead of a gable end was demanded for a building less than three bays wide, the cornice itself or the attic was raised in the centre. This also served to hide the ridge or to enable a hatch to be made for easier use of the hoisting beam.

Apart from the emphasis on the straight or raised cornice, the rather flat façades of the houses were characterized by the decorated central element. This middle bay was often emphasized by a double perron, a doorpost-framing and decorations around the middle window on the first floor. With richer houses these surrounds continued upwards to the cornice. There are many canal houses, especially from the Louis XIV period, which are decorated in such a way as to give the impression that they are palaces. The *Grachtenboek* of 1767 with drawings by Caspar Philips of almost 1500 houses is an important source for checking whether they are still in their original state.

The façades of the bigger houses are mostly of sandstone, and cheaper brick is used for the simpler neck-gables and bell-gables, although Abraham van der Hart did use brick for his Armenhuis and Maagdenhuis around 1780. These were, however, commissions in which great simplicity was aimed at. Towards the end of the century the brick front was often plastered, creating a smooth, monumental effect.

The window, which in the eighteenth century was to become an important compositional element in the façades, had been designed since the Middle Ages as a cross made up of a mullion and transom. However, after 1710 the French sliding sash window made its entrance. The division of the window changed in the course of the century. Most houses were given windows with bigger window-panes.

The interior became lighter through the use of the tall sash window and through the increasing use of stucco ceilings. The interior, in contrast to the seventeenth century, was designed more as a unity. The rooms were no longer regarded as being separated from each other. The hall and the staircase were given a central place.

Daniel Marot

The enormous influence of the French building styles, clearly visible in the interiors, reached Amsterdam mainly through Daniel Marot, who lived here from 1705 till 1717. In the following years the undeniable influence of his Louis XIV style can be seen in the stucco and façade designs such as those of the decorator-architects Jan van Logteren and Frans Blanchard. In the forties the fairly heavy baroque shapes of Marot were used in a more playful way by the brothers Hans Jacob and Hendrick Husly.

In de eighteenth century there was no clear leader among the architects. However, Jacob Otten Husly, the cousin of the brothers Husly mentioned above, played an important role after 1750. His design for Felix Meritis in 1788 with its Corinthian half columns, was an exceptional building for Amsterdam. During the Louis periods in Amsterdam, pillars or pilasters, along the entire façade, were hardly used, in contrast to France. This changed around 1770. Herengracht 527 is a very early example of this. This return to classical motifs, known in France as the Louis XVI style, had little influence in Amsterdam and only led to a tightening of the design language. Thus, the Armenhuis and the Maagdenhuis were built in a restrained, simple style by Abraham van der Hart, city architect in the last quarter of the century. The only decorations were to be found in the pediments, by Anthonie Ziesenis, the most important sculptor of that period.

Middenweg 72
1st quarter 18th century – Frankendaal

This country house consists of a main building flanked by a stable and a coach house. The brickwork front elevation has a timber cornice and balustrade. The garden, behind which are the municipal nurseries has a fountain by Ignatius van Logteren (1714) and an entrance gate (1783) with the coat of arms of J. Gildemeester.

201 *tram 9* □ *(gardens only)*

Kromboomsloot 22
1714 Heilige Geest

After a hundred years as a Roman Catholic church the building was repurchased by the Armenian community in 1986. When restoration is completed the building will also serve as a cultural centre. The doorway with an Armenian text and a carving of a lamb and the steps are noteworthy.

202 *centre* ■

Herengracht 554
1716

The original 17th century house was rebuilt in 1716 and was given an attic and two statues on the straight cornice. The centre is emphasized by a richly decorated balcony and the double perron – both added as part of the restoration.

203 *centre* ■

Herengracht 539
Jean Coulon (attrib.)
1718

This property was altered in 1718 by G. Corver, probably after an original design for Herengracht 433 by Coulon. The monumental sandstone façade is only three bays wide and has a balcony supported by female figures and, above the cornice, a blind attic with a raised central section and statues.

204 *centre* ■

1e Weteringdwarsstraat 11-43
1721-1731   Grill's Hofje

These pleasant almshouses for elderly women have nine identical bell-gables on the street side. Pairs of houses share a common timber entrance stair. The street at the rear is reached through the middle house (nr. 19) and has six more houses and a clock of 1727. There is also a trustees' room.

205 *centre* □

Kloveniersburgwal 6-8
1722   Abraham and Isaac

Formerly number 4 had a similar neck-gable with a carving of Jacob at the top. Now Isaac (nr. 8) alone looks at patriarch Abraham (nr. 6) who stares straight ahead. These two properties with their common timber front and separate single-bay brickwork façades were restored in 1980.

206 *centre* ■

Nieuwe Herengracht 6-18
1723   Corvershof

Almshouses founded by J. Corver and S. Trip for poverty-stricken elderly couples, now part of the Amstelhof. The central element in the façade, bounded by two Ionic pilasters, is closed by a segmental pediment in which an allegory of charity is accompanied by an eagle bearing the coat of arms of the 'hof'.

207   *centre* ■

Keizersgracht 444-446
1725

This richly decorated baroque façade does not look very Dutch. The two properties were combined in 1758 and were altered several times. The rendered sandstone elevation ends with a cornice with attic and centrepiece. Unfortunately, the original double entrance perron has been removed. Now part of the Public Library.

208   *centre* ■

Lange Leidsedwarsstraat 129-131
1726

Double neck-gable with unusual scrolls (volutes) with an acanthus motif, under which is a tablet depicting a cow's head and the year. The property on the left is still in its original condition. Four bell-gables on nrs. 148-154 were built fifty years later.

209   *centre* ■

Herengracht 520
1726-1727

This property was completely altered. A façade with cornice, attic and alliance coats of arms was added as well as decorated windows and a door with Ionic pilasters and curved architrave. The original window divisions have been removed. The entrance stair with its mouldings and railings is particularly fine.

210 *centre* ■

Prins Hendrikkade 133
1727

Residence in the Louis XIV style with sandstone facing and richly decorated cornice and attic. The cornice has an arched central section flanked by tritons blowing horns, a Mercury staff and two corner vases. Only the centre window on the first floor has a decorated surround. The building now houses a fashion school.

211 *centre* ■

Diemerszeedijk 27
Cornelis van der Hoeven
1727   Gemeenlandshuis

A restored, plain, dignified building with corner pilasters on a simple façade. The entrance was originally more richly decorated. The interior has carvings by Pierre le Normant and plasterwork by Christiaan Wittenbeeker. Now Hoogheemraadschap Amstelland (polder authority).

212 *tram 3-10* □ *(on request)*

Herengracht 284
1728   Huize Van Brienen

Originally built in the 17th century, this property was rebuilt in the Regency style in 1728. It came into possession of the Van Brienen family in 1781. Since 1932 it has been owned by the Hendrick de Keyser Society, an organization which is responsible for the purchase and restoration of many properties. Sandstone façade with a straight cornice, attic and frieze with small windows. The interior and the summer-house are well worth viewing.

213   *centre* □ *(on request)*

Keizersgracht 606-608
1730

Two neck-gables in the Louis XIV style. Among the largest in Amsterdam. Nr. 610 had an identical façade until 1790. The gables are capped by crests. The hoisting-beam opening is decorated. Nr. 606 has an early 19th century door and a bench on the perron.

214   *centre* ■

Herengracht 475
Hans Jacob Husly (attrib.)
1730

House with monumental sandstone façade in Louis XIV style with a fine doorpost-framing and two female figures on the first floor. The façade is closed by a straight cornice with attic and balustrade. The house has a splendid interior in which the hall and staircase occupy a prominent position with important plasterwork and sculpture.

215   *centre* □ *(on request)*

Nieuwe Keizersgracht 28-44
Daniel Marot
1732   Van Brants-Rushofje

Almshouses founded by Chr. van Brants for Evangelical Lutheran women. The brick façade with its decorated centre element and double stairs has a relief depicting Charity above the cornice. Above the entrance is a eulogy to the founder. The 'hofje' has a fine trustees' room.

216 *centre* ■

Herengracht 495
Jean Coulon
1739

Original 17th century façade rebuilt for Jan Six. The balcony with its wrought-iron railings and the text *Omnia orta occidunt* dates from 1775. The stone façade is closed by a cornice, attic and balustrade.

217 *centre* ■

Oudezijds Voorburgwal 215-217
2nd quarter 18th century

The façade has a blind attic, richly embellished in the centre above a straight cornice. The form of the balustrade is especially interesting. The illusion of curving inwards above the outer bays is caused by the downward bending. The cornice has decorated consoles and hoisting beams. There are small windows in the frieze.

218 *centre* ■

Herengracht 164
1750-1775

Four-bay façade with a straight cornice and attic. Above the attic, which is treated as a balustrade and centrepiece, are four vases. The doorpost-framing with its Ionic pilasters is original.

219 *centre* ■

Nieuwe Herengracht 143
1750

The bluestone façade has a raised cornice in which an attic window has been placed. Below the cornice are plain consoles and rectangles. The door and window mouldings are in compar-atively low relief. The elevation is bounded by banded corner pilasters.

220 *centre* ■

Nieuwe Herengracht 103
1751

This originally 17th century property has a particularly fine entranceway with sophisticated ironwork railings to the steps and a rococo doorpost-framing. The bluestone façade is closed by a cornice under which are fanciful consoles. On the first floor is a fine room with a double fireplace.

221 *centre* ■

Jonas Daniel Meijerplein
G.F. Maybaum
1752   Nieuwe Synagoge

This austere, symmetrical building has a balustrade with a semicircular centrepiece above the cornice and a small dome on the roof. The entrance has inbedded Ionic columns. The building was closed in 1936 but has now been restored (A. Cahen/Premsela Vonk) and since 1987 has become, together with the adjoining synagogue, the Joods Historisch Museum (Jewish Historical Museum).

222   centre □

Herengracht 39
1753   Gouda

In the 18th century warehouses were usually much simpler than their predecessors. This property, however, has a richly decorated bell-gable. Nr. 37 is again much plainer. Both have unusual, timber lower fronts. This indicates a combined function as a storage and office space.

223   centre ■

Kloveniersburgwal 72
Pieter Rendorp
1754   Oudemanhuis

These former almshouses for elderly men and women have belonged to Amsterdam University since 1876. There are four wings enclosing an almost square courtyard. The elevations to this courtyard are in brickwork with stone porticos capped by triangular pediments. The city's coat of arms is displayed on the north pediment.

224   centre □ (access via **242**)

Keizersgracht 546
1760

A good example of a Louis XV bell-gable with playful rococo volutes and a wide crest. The third floor still has its hoisting hatch. The window division is early 19th century. Little else has been altered.

225 *centre* ■

Roomolenstraat 11
1760

This property is unusual in that it is a neck-gable in Louis XV style. Usually the bell-gable was used for this playful ornamentation as the neck-gable was less suitable.

226 *centre* ■

Keizersgracht 224
1765   Saxenburg

Sandstone façade with four bays, closed by a straight cornice and attic with raised centre and decorative vases. There is a double entrance perron and the door and first floor window have moulded surrounds. The interior still has its 18th century hall and staircase and a room with plasterwork.

227 *centre* □

Prinsengracht 300
1767 't Vosje

This house, which was restored in 1959, received its name from the 17th century furrier's house on the same site called De Witte Vos. Above the two doors in the timber lower front is a red fox with a bird in its mouth. Below the hoisting beam at the top of this fine bell-gable is another fox.

228 *centre* ■

Herengracht 493
1770

The austere façade of this originally 17th century house is a good example of the late Louis XV style. The plaster-work in the interior dates from the 18th century. The sandstone façade with its pediment and attic has had its original window divisions restored.

229 *centre* ■

Herengracht 527
1770

Extremely early example of a Louis XVI façade with Ionic pilasters over the first and second storeys and a pediment with an eagle. Only the tall, hipped roof remains of the original 17th century house. The windows were altered around 1800.

230 *centre* ■

Alexanderplein
Cornelis Rauws
1770 Muiderpoort

Formerly one of the city gates. A classical building with a central dome and lantarn. Above Doric columns the pediment has a relief carving of the Amsterdam coat of arms by A. Ziesenis.

231 *centre* ■

Nieuwe Keizersgracht 120
Coenraad Hoeneker
1771 Luthers Diaconiehuis

Restrained, dignified building almost without decoration, apart from the pediment with its clock. J. Otten Husly probably participated in the building operations. It is now the Luthers Verpleeghuis (Lutheran Nursing Home), which is inscribed above the door. There is a fine trustees' room.

232 *centre* ■

Herengracht 182
Ludwig Friedrich Druck
1772 Zonnewijser

The name Sundial and the sun on the façade are derived from the original house. The house was built for Van Brienen and has a sandstone façade with straight cornice and attic. The interior has plasterwork ceilings dating from 1772. The double entrance perron was reconstructed during the restoration of 1972. The house is sometimes known as Huize Van Brienen II **(213)**.

233 *centre* ■

Nieuwe Keizersgracht 94
**1774   Occo's Hof/Gesticht van
        Barmhartigheid**

The pediment above the stone portico of this austere Louis XVI façade, displays the coat of arms of the founder, C.E. Occo. The 'hofje', formally for poor widows and spinsters has a trustees' room and a fine garden court. It was extended and modernized in the 19th century when the chapel was also demolished.

234   *centre* ■

Geldersekade 8
1775   Tabaksvat

Louis XVI façade with austere, straight cornice. There are garlands between the consoles and an attic window in the centre. The frieze is higher than usual to accommodate this attic window. Above the door is a relief showing two baskets and a cask and the text *Tabaksvat* (Tobacco cask).

235   *centre* ■

Prinsenstraat 12
c. 1775

An unusual house in that it is the only surviving example of a Louis XVI neckgable in Amsterdam. On the top is a carving of a beehive. There is now a shop in the 19th century lower front.

236   *centre* ■

Middenweg 4-6/Ringdijk
Caspar Philips
1777   Rechthuis

The Courthouse of the former independent district of Watergraafsmeer also served as an inn. This brick building has Doric columns next to the entrance and garlands around the middle window. The portico is crowned by a pediment and by a turret on the roof. The original steps and lanterns have been removed.

237   *tram 9* ■

Roeterstraat 2
Abraham van der Hart
1779-1782   Armen-Werkhuis

This present-day nursing home was designed as a home for criminals and the poor: both of which groups are depicted in the tympanum with the patroness of the city in a relief by A. Ziesenis. This dignified building with its almost complete lack of ornamentation has a classical feel about it. The building was praised for its light, air and hygiene and was imitated in the Maagdenhuis **(240)**.

238   *tram 7* ■

Vierwindendwarsstraat 1
1781   Drie Gekroonde Haringen

A house which is freestanding on three sides. The sloping roof-planes are carried round the three open sides. There is a straight cornice and corner chimneys which were reconstructed as part of the restorations. The original glazing bars have also been reinstalled, reinforcing the restrained dignity of this simple, brick building. The three crowned herrings are depicted in the doorpost-framing, which is also original.

239   *tram 3* ■

Spui
Abraham van der Hart
1783-1787   Maagdenhuis

This accommodation for Roman Catholic orphaned girls was, like the Armen Werkhuis **(238)**, to be 'free of pomp and adornment but sound and strong'. The interior of this brick building with its stone entrance and tympanum by A. Ziesenis has been altered and modernized. It has been owned by the University of Amsterdam since 1961.

240   *centre* □

Amstel 56
Abraham van der Hart
1785   Franse Schouwburg

This taut, austere building was formerly the French Theatre. A small pediment above the dormer, and the straight cornice are the only ornaments. Van der Hart introduced a new type of window from France. It had larger panes than had previously been usual. For a hundred years the building has been occupied by the Kleine Komedie Theatre.

241   *centre* □

Kloveniersburgwal
A. Ziesenis
1786   Oudemanhuispoort

The Oudemanhuispoort provides access to the university building and to a second-hand book market. The sculpture by Ziesenis portrays a maiden offering a cornucopia to two aged figures. The gate on the Oudezijds Achterburgwal (1754) has an arched pediment with a pair of spectacles symbolizing old age.

242   *centre* □

Keizersgracht 324
Jacob Otten Husly
1788   Felix Meritis

This imposing building with its four sturdy inbedded columns was the office of the Felix Meritis Fellowship, the cultural centre of Amsterdam. The decorations on the façade portray the various arts. Inside is an oval room which later served as the model for the Kleine Zaal of the Concertgebouw **(339)**. Most of the building had to be rebuilt after the fire of 1932.

243 *centre* □

Nieuwe Herengracht 20
1789-1790   Bestedelingenhuis/
Amstelrank

From the poem above the entrance it would appear that the building was paid for from the legacy of Johanna van Mekeren-Bontekoning. Completely freestanding, the building is characterized by its great austerity (both outside and inside). This in contrast to the adjacent Corvershof **(207)**. It is now the Amstelhof's staff residence.

244 *centre*

Singel 145
1790

Simple late 18th century bell-gable; noteworthy for its unusual Louis XVI decoration. The door is original.

245 *centre* ■

Herengracht 40
Jacob Otten Husly (attrib.)
1790-1791

Calm, distinguished building, constructed by T.A. van Iddekinge. One of the few late 18th century residential properties. The wide sandstone façade is closed by a straight cornice with consoles and rosettes. The semicircular fanlights on the main floor are noteworthy.

246 *centre* ■

Kloveniersburgwal 50
Abraham van der Hart/
B.W.H. Ziesenis
1792-1793 Hersteld Evangelisch
Lutherse Gemeente

Only the classical façade of this church, which has been disused since 1950, is still intact. The relief in the pediment is by A. Ziesenis, whose son was also involved in the construction of the building. The central pavilion with rusticated base has six Ionic pilasters, carrying a cornice and pediment. It is now owned by the Rijksmarechaussee (military police).

247 *centre* ■

Herengracht 502
Abraham van der Hart
1792 Deutzhuis

This originally 17th century house was rebuilt by Abraham van der Hart for C. Deutz van Assendelft. The emphasis in the severe façade with its straight cornice is on the central entrance whose two Doric colomns support the marble balcony. There is still a room in the Louis XVI style. Official residence of the mayor since 1927.

248 *centre* ■

Nineteenth century

In the nineteenth century as in the eighteenth century Dutch architects mainly followed developments abroad. Nineteenth century Amsterdam can be approached in two different ways: as an isolated period, with its jumble of styles and strange, new building commissions such as stations, circuses and industrial palaces, or as a period in which specifically after about 1860 the foundations of the period 1900-1940 are laid, the period in which Dutch architecture played a leading role for a short while. For a foreigner the second approach is perhaps more interesting than the first one, for, generally speaking, he will search in vain for the spectacle that nineteenth century towns like Paris, Vienna, Brussels and London have to offer. The post – 1895 economic revival – hesitant in the sixties, then strong again after 1875 and again after a crisis towards the end of the eighties, came too late for this. It is not possible to detect a similar sharp split between the first and the second half in most European capitals.

The development of Amsterdam had stagnated until 1860. There was no population growth, no migration and hardly any movement in the social structure. There were hardly any economic developments. From 1830 onwards advantage was taken of the profits, yielded by the so-called forced farming system (Cultuurstelsel) on Java. More buildings were demolished than built. The gable ends of houses were truncated by the hundred and, in the interest of cheapness as well as under the influence of 'classicism', they were provided with extremely simple straight cornices.

Louis Napoleon

One can hardly speak of architecture under these circumstances. It is true that, during the French occupation, King Louis Napoleon, the man who turned the town hall into the Koninklijk Paleis (Royal Palace), did as much as possible for the arts and especially for architecture. He enabled young architects to study on a grant in Paris and Rome. In their few large projects, these 'pensionnaires' (Suys, Zocher, De Greef) were in fact the only architects to show any affinity with international developments from the 1820's onwards. From sheer necessity all superfluous decoration was left out in their work. As all religious denominations had had freedom of worship since the French period, a number of churches were also built during this period. However, production was still low in this field in comparison with the second half of the century when, especially since the rehabilitation of the episcopal hierarchy in the Roman-Catholic church (1853), the silhouette of Amsterdam was enriched with a great number of church towers. From the fifties onwards a modest impulse was also given to building activity by so-called philanthropical working-class housing. This attempted to improve the appalling living conditions in the Jordaan and other working-class areas, which were considered a danger to public health, by building large estates, amply provided with light and air.

Paleis voor Volksvlijt

Foreign travellers visiting Amsterdam in the 1860's and 1870's were surprised at the apathy and phlegmatism with which the city allowed itself to be surpassed by other capitals and by various industrial 'boom-towns'. The upturn was symbolized by the Paleis voor Volksvlijt (1857-1864, destroyed by fire 1929), one of the strangest glass and iron industrial palaces that Europe has seen. Inspired by the Crystal Palace of the Great Exhibition of 1851, it was the brainchild of Dr. Samuel Sarphati who is known as 'the founder of modern Amsterdam'. Most of the large building projects in the second half of the nineteenth century, the period of flourishing liberal citizenship, were the results of the efforts of individuals or private companies: Artis Zoo, Vondelpark, Wester-gasfabriek, the Stadsschouwburg etc. The architect of the Paleis voor Volksvlijt, which was crowned with a dome, and of the stately, still existing Amstelhotel, was C. Outshoorn. He is considered the first modern architect who introduced an office system for his enterprise, like the engineers had already done before him. Partly self-taught and partly educated by a railway engineer, his special virtue was that he introduced a liberal scale of building and design to the Amsterdam of that period. With a sidelong glance at the French 'modern renaissance', as the architecture of the Second Empire was known, his work showed an eclecticism which was somewhat lacking in direction.

P.J.H. Cuypers

P.J.H. Cuypers also derived his inspiration for the most part from France, albeit from the radical camp of Viollet-le-Duc. When he started, in 1876, with the designs for the Centraal Station and the Rijksmuseum, both in what he himself understood to be in a national style, for a quarter of a century he had been gaining experience in the building of several Catholic churches in the south of the Netherlands, most of them in Romanesque or early-Gothic style. Cuypers was regarded by many architects of the first part of the twentieth century as the grandfather of modern building (Berlage, of course, being the father) because he re-thought the basic principles of architecture, with the phrase he borrowed from Viollet-le-Duc as a motto above his work: 'toute forme qui n'est pas indiquée par la structure doit être repoussée' (all form which is not indicated by structure must be repulsed). Much of what took place in the period of 1900-1940 in Dutch architecture is hardly conceivable without the work of Cuypers; not only because of the emphasis on structural rationalism borrowed from Gothic church-building, but also because of his concept of a Gesamtkunstwerk which, from ground plan and structure to the tiniest detail should be governed by one regulating principle. There is an almost straight line linking the Rijksmuseum to Berlage's Koopmansbeurs (1898-1903). It is striking that both buildings tell an elaborate story – the one about Dutch (art) history, the other about the history of Amsterdam as a merchant city. Both architects were advised by sympathising men of letters. And, in addition, both followed the architecture and the icono-graphy of the Stadhuis on the Dam.

Dutch neo-Renaissance

Neo-Renaissance too, participated in the revival of architecture in the late nineteenth century. The Maatschappij ter Bevordering der Bouwkunst (Dutch Society of Architects, founded in 1842) supported eclecticism as the more or less official line after 1850. From this the Dutch neo-Renaissance developed slowly but gradually. In the 1880's and 1890's it was the dominant school of architecture. As early as the 1860's I. Gosschalk (a pupil of Gottfried Semper), was an advocate of this style. He pleaded against the diluted carpenter's classicism, against Cuyper's neo-Gothic style and against the eclectic styles of the Maatschappij. Like Cuypers his point of departure was the indigenous Dutch brick style of the sixteenth and early seventeenth century.
Next to the Maatschappij a more artistic unrestrained society existed, called Architectura et Amicitia. The central figure was Jan L. Springer. He was a bohemian, more renowned for his French-style sketches and admired by the younger neo-Renaissance architects for his terrific architectural fantasies.
Ed. Cuypers (a pupil of his uncle P.J.H. Cuypers) provided the link between the late nineteenth century and the more individual expressionism of the Amsterdam School architecture. Just before the turn of the century he abandoned neo-Renaissance. Through his work several important influences reached Dutch architecture, especially those of Norman Shaw and the modern English country-house style (which was also noticeable in the work of A. Salm). In 1899 Ed. Cuypers took on the fifteen-year-old Michel de Klerk in his new studio in the Jan Luykenstraat. De Klerk left in 1910 when his style had already been shaped for the greater part.

Art Nouveau

Art Nouveau is almost entirely absent from Amsterdam with the exception of several tiled tableaux, shop fronts and insurance buildings. It was rejected as being too 'decorative'. The variant was the Nieuwe Kunst which was more adapted to the old Dutch virtues of truth and craftmanship in construction. The American Hotel by W. Kromhout, a member of the influential, but in the 1890's still mainly theoretically active Architectura group, provided an interim climax. Within this group, Berlage was strongly influenced by some austerely designed competition entries by K.P.C. de Bazel. Neither were the developments in modern American architecture to remain unnoticed. The most important activities of Berlage, Kromhout and De Bazel, however, took place after the turn of the century.

*Paleis voor Volksvlijt and
Sarphatistraat, seen
from Amstel Hotel*

Prinsengracht 436
J. de Greef
1825-1829   Paleis van Justitie

De Greef, city architect from 1820-1834, rebuilt the Aalmoezeniersweeshuis (Almoners' Orphanage) as a Court of Justice around two courtyards. The interior and the hall have been well preserved. Semicircular arches to the entrance as at the Stadhuis on the Dam Square **(147)**. Sober classicism with pavilions emphasized by pilasters and balustrades. Empire style windows.

301   *centre* □

Groenburgwal 42
J. Jansen (church)
1827-1829   English Episcopal
                       Church

Early example of Romantic Gothic on one of the most picturesque canals. Former Draper's Hall converted into a church in 1827. In 1829 the vicarage, in front of the actual church and formerly the home of Hendrick de Keyser, was given a new façade, probably designed by an unknown English architect. With its orange-red brickwork it fits in well with its sourroundings. Until the 1860's neo-Gothicism was purely decorative.

302   *centre* ■

Kadijksplein
J. de Greef/C.W.M. Klijn/G. Moele
1827   Former Rijks-Entrepot

Viewed from the Plantage Doklaan an impressive row of different warehouses, mostly 19th century. In 1857 51 existing warehouses were bought by the State and partly rebuilt. Thirty-three new warehouses were built and onto Kadijksplein administrative buildings were added in an austere Doric style. The colonade was later bricked up. The block was recently converted into apartments by J. van Stigt.

303   *centre* □ *(grounds only)*

Singel 460
M.G. Tétar van Elven
1837   Concertzaal Odeon

Despite restricted entry and the paint-work, the concert hall on the first floor is worth a visit. In the 1840's and 1850's, the classicist Tétar van Elven dominated the architectural scene – although he had few commissions. The parabolic shape of the auditorium, intended to give good acoustics, was calculated by a teacher from the Jordaan.

304   *centre □ (access via **156**)*

Waterlooplein 205
T.F. Suys/J. van Straaten
1837-1841   St. Antonius van Padua/
Mozes en Aäronkerk

A classical building, originally built-in on both sides. Designed by the Fleming Suys (Prix de Rome, a pupil of Percier), and executed by Van Straaten. Finally it was built with three-quarter round pilasters, because of city regulations which forced the architect to reduce the portico. Wooden towers inspired by St. Sulpice in Paris. During restoration (1969) all the woodwork and sandstone was painted a sandstone colour.

305   *centre □*

Haarlemmerplein 50
C. Alewijn/C.W.M. Klijn
1840   Willemspoort

Neoclassical gatehouse for the assessment and collection of local taxes. Corinthian columns, not completely accurate as the masons misjudged the entasis; hence the over-tapering under the astragal. Capitals by the sculptor De Koningh who also worked on those of the Madeleine in Paris. Restored and converted to dwellings in 1986.

306   *centre ■*

Dam/Nieuwezijds Voorburgwal
M.G. Tétar van Elven
1844

Six monumental, bronze-coloured, cast-iron lamp-posts, richly decorated with acanthus leaves and winged lions. Tétar van Elven is described as a 'gifted man' who had little chance to develop his talents during this period of low building activity.

307 *centre*

Houtmanstraat 1-27/Planciusstraat
P.J. Hamer
1854-1856   Modelwoningblok Ver-
eeniging ten behoeve
der Arbeidersklasse

'Philanthropic' housing for the working classes (see **314**). Equal window heights and characteristic access by way of centrally placed well-lit, staircases. A large, subtly composed block, especially on the Houtmanstraat: seven pavilions divided into three types, attached in different ways; window types vary according to the size of the dwelling unit.

308 *tram 3* ■

Keizersgracht 676
A.N. Godefroy
1854-1856   Nieuwe Walenkerk/
Adventskerk

Hall church with galleries on cast-iron columns, with graceful lanterns. Sandstone façade complete with lanterns echoing the adjoining 17th century façades. Rusticated classical base below and round Romanesque arch style above. Lombardian arched moulding and heavy corner buttresses (altered in 1862 after fire). Godefroy was one of the major architects of (third-quarter) nineteenth century eclecticism.

309 *centre* □

Rokin 112
J.H. Leliman
1855   Arti et Amicitiae

An unorthodox building for its time,
influenced by Leliman's teacher in
Paris H. Labrouste. The rather restrained façade reflects a logical subdivision
of the spaces behind: a blasphemy
against the 'Beaux Arts' lessons of his
(first) teacher M.G. Tétar van Elven.
Sculpture by F. Stracké. Old Dutch
staircase by H.P. Berlage/A.C Bleys
(1894). Houses an artists' society.

310   *centre* □ *(Gallery & staircase)*

Keizersgracht 452
C. Outshoorn
1860   Woonhuis Fuld

17th century property, altered to a
classical residence with Baroque
decoration and heavy central emphasis
above the double perron. Ornamentation in painted terracotta. This is one of
the last of a two-hundred-year, unbro-
ken tradition of Italian and French influenced stately canal houses, beginning with Vingboons and Van Campen
and ending with Outshoorn.

311   *centre* ■

Haarlemmerstraat 126-128
P.J.H. Cuypers
1860-1863/1887-1889
Posthoornkerk

Gothic-Romanesque transept basilica
with cloverleaf choir, inspired by the
German Rhineland. The silhouette
makes it clear that Cuypers was
searching for a combination of a basilica and a centralized church early in his
career. The two tiers of galleries in the
narrow interior, with its subtle polychromy are noteworthy; a reference to
the original secret church-building period. In 1989 the interior was partly
turned into offices by A. van Stigt.

312   *centre* ■

Keizersgracht 609
C. Outshoorn
1861-1863   Museum Fodor

A conversion of 'Spook'warehouse into a gallery for art collector C.J. Fodor. Large room at rear with skylight, now completely modernized. Richly decorated façade in Bentheimer sandstone. Remarkably narrow-looking windows.

313   *centre* □

Westerstraat 195-215/327-405
Lijnbaansgracht 63-65
P.J. Hamer
1862-1864

Tenement blocks for 'philanthropic' working-class housing societies based on English precedents, often initiated by businessmen influenced by the Protestant Revival (Bible tract on Lijnbaansgracht 64), with capital retention and a low rate of interest. Eclecticism: classical articulation with pavilions and rusticated buttresses; Romanesque and Gothic detailing. Converted and restored in 1985.

314   *centre* ■

Prof. Tulpplein 1
C. Outshoorn
1863-1867   Amstelhotel

Outshoorn succeeded here in giving the Amstel, together with the Hogesluis (bridge), the metropolitan allure, for which Sarphati had striven. At a later date an extra storey was added to the French Second Empire wings, thus destroying the proportion between the pavilions and the wings.

315   *centre* □

Amsteldijk 273
J.D & L.P. Zocher
1869/1891-1892   Zorgvlied

The oldest section of the cemetery, on the right-hand side, was landscaped in 1869 and has an open, orderly arrangement. Carré **(337)** the circus family's tomb (J. P. F. van Rossem and W.J. Vuyk), the huge 'East Indian' Dorrepaal family grave and the rather sentimental grave of the banker Rosenthal are worth a visit.

316   *tram 25* □

Oude Turfmarkt 127
W.A. Froger
1865-1869   Nederlandse Bank

Designed as a conscious contrast to the National Bank in Brussels, which was considered too exuberant. Much attention was paid to the vertical accents in the pavilions, leading to a particularly successful balance. Curve in the building line echoed by rounded corners to the pavilion. Colour contrast in the façade achieved by the use of Bremer stone and Bentheimer stone. Now houses the Allard Pierson Museum.

317   *centre* □

Plantage Lepellaan 6
W. & J.L. Springer
1874

Sumptuous and beautifully situated urban villa with garden in a quiet part of the Plantage. Mixture of renaissance and classicism. Red brickwork, Escauzine stone, sculptural ornamentation in reconstructed Portland cement based stone. The bronze-painted statues and vases in the niches are zink: on the left a man with a sickle, on the right a woman holding her hands over a cooking pot. This suggests a possible winter and summer house.

318   *tram 9* ■

Vondelstraat 73-75/77-79
P.J.H. Cuypers
1876/1881

77-79 – Double house with floor plan symmetrically mirrored but with a super-structure of two pitched roofs at right angles to each other. Cuypers' former house (nr. 77) has an altered entrance and, on the left, some later additions. Bracket under bay window derived from Viollet-le-Duc, as is the rationalist planning. Sgrafitto tiled tableaux showing: left, the architect, centre, the mason and, on the right, the jealous critic.

319 *tram 1* ■

Vondelpark
J.D. & L.P. Zocher/J.J. Kerbert
1865-1877

By Amsterdam standards a large open space. The oldest part by J.D. Zocher has calm lines and broad perspectives, in the early English landscape style. Pavilion, now Film Museum (P.J. & W. Hamer, 1881). Statue of the poet Vondel (L. Royer), pedestal (P.J.H. Cuypers, 1867). Monumental entrance railings on the Stadhouderskade (A. Linneman, 1883). Round teahouse-functionalism (H.A.J. Baanders, 1937).

320 *tram 1, 2, 5* □

Plantage Middenlaan 60
G.B. Salm
1878

In the Plantage there are many examples of 'carpenter's classicism' or 'plasterer's style' in which cheap and shoddy structures are hidden behind rendered façades: Salm, an architect who built soundly, shows that with good proportions and appropriate detailing even stuccoed architecture can please, in spite of a restricted budget.

321 *tram 9* ■

Vossiusstraat 1-15
I. Gosschalk
1879

Successful example of speculative building for the better-off. Fifteen terraced houses, in plan and section resembling an 18th century palace, incorporating two wings and pavilions. Louis XVI ornament with a meander, palmettes, Vitruvian Scroll, etc. Few vertical accents due to situation, immediately opposite Vondelpark.

322 *tram 1, 2, 5* ■

Reguliersgracht 57-59/63
I. Gosschalk
1879/c. 1882

Two façades with a great deal of carpentry. On the left the German inspired façade with Old Dutch shopfront which has been so well publicised. The façade on the right is more interesting, a combination of Old Dutch with Old English and Queen Anne. It is possible that Gosschalk was acquainted with these styles through the work of Norman Shaw.

323 *centre* ■

Vondelstraat 120
P.J.H. Cuypers
1872-1880   Heilige Hartkerk/
Vondelkerk

Cuypers's masterpiece. Interior plundered during vacancy (1979-1985). The alterations and new function make experience of interior difficult but did make possible the preservation of the church. The church is the centre of an oval square – also designed by Cuypers. The building combines an octagonal centralized structure with a longitudinal axis. The Gothic Liebfrauenkirche in Trier and the Baroque church of Vierzehnheiligen are possible sources. (Interior A. van Stigt, 1986)

324 *tram 1* □

Keizersgracht 508
A.C. Bleys
1881

Picturesque, finely detailed corner property in a free neo-Renaissance eclectic style. The splayed corner with an oriel-tower is the so-called German solution which, in the 19th century, was preferred to the native solution with two gable ends standing at right-angles to each other.

325 *centre* ■

Vondelstraat 140
A.L. van Gendt
1881 Hollandse Manege

Passage, vestibule and beautifully plastered manege with elegant open iron roofing, in what was formerly known as Viennese renaissance and nowadays as International Classicism. Sources: Spanische Reitschule and possibly the Dianabad (K. Etzel, 1842) in Vienna. Large false brackets under the tie-rods and zinc horses' heads. 153 Stalls and boxes (now altered and partially demolished) integrally supplied by the St. Pancras Iron Work Co. London.

326 *tram 1* □

Plantage Middenlaan 53
G.B. & A. Salm
1882 Aquarium Natura Artis
        Magistra

On the outside: the Aquarium with monumental peristyle and red sandstone base (1882), the storage buildings in chalet style on the Plantage Muidergracht (1875, 1890); the former library and museum at Plantage Middenlaan 45 (1868);
41-43 – former main building with its rich cast-iron door and window bars (J. van Maurik, 1855). Entrance kiosks and railing crowned with zinc eagles (1854). Director's house (J.F. Klinkhamer, 1897).

327 *tram 9* □

Stadhouderskade 41
P.J.H. Cuypers
1877-1885   Rijksmuseum

Built for three purposes: museum of
national history, national art and the
education of artists. Hence the elaborate iconographic programme in the
interior and on the exterior. In spite of
the majestic Gothic silhouette and fine
proportions, the strength of this 'national renaissance' styled building lies
in the detailing rather than in the handling of space. This is especially evident in the plan which is based on Van
Campen's Stadhuis **(147),** but misses
the latter's compact handling of
space.

328   *centre* □

Singel 446
A. Tepe
1881   Krijtberg

Three-aisled neo-Gothic transeptal
basilica of great height. The church is
wider at the chancel end than at the
narrow street frontage. Tepe worked in
a more archeological Gothic than Cuypers and made little use of modern
techniques such as structural ironwork. The church is unique in that its
interior decorations have almost completely been preserved. Extremely rich
polychromy.

329   *centre* □

Amstel
W. Springer/B. de Greef
1884   Blauwbrug

Like the Hogesluis over the Amstel at
the Sarphatistraat inspired by the
Alexander III bridge in Paris, but with
an adapted iconography. Fine sculptures on the central piers; balustrade in
white lime-stone (Comblanchien),
cast-iron railings, pedestals in Escauzine stone and columns in highly pol-
ished red Swedish granite on which
stand bronze lanterns and the imperial
crown of Amsterdam.

330   *centre* □

Prinsengracht 739-741
Ed. Cuypers
1884   Melkinrichting

In the 1880's nearly all the important architects who had been born in the 1850's – Ed. Cuypers, Berlage, Van Arkel and J.L. Springer – were working in the Dutch renaissance, whose decorative, picturesque versatility was quickly seized upon to be combined with other styles, such as the timber style used here.

331   *centre* ■

Haarlemmerweg 10
I. Gosschalk
1885   Imperial Continental Gas Association/Westergasfabriek

The *zuiveringshal* is one of the most surprising buildings from the age of the 'neo' styles. An applied architecture in freely designed neo-renaissance which is both rationalist and picturesque. Ascending arched corbel courses and narrow high windows make the fronts look slightly Romanesque. The extensive original Westergasfabriek was U-shaped and built around a water tower. A large part was demolished in the 1960's.

332   *tram 10* ■

Kalverstraat 152
H.P. Berlage/Th. Sanders
1886   Focke & Meltzer

Berlage's first large commission, in association with his partner Th. Sanders. Venetian renaissance building with medallions in the spandrels depicting Palissy, Luca della Robbia, Wedgewood and the Crabeth brothers – masters of glass and faience. The large window-panes behind freestanding granite columns are noteworthy. The roof storey on the Spui side is a later addition.

333   *centre* □

Stationsplein
P.J.H. Cuypers/A.L. van Gendt/
L.J. Eijmer
1882-1889   Centraal Station

Built on a specially constructed island,
which fenced Amsterdam off from the
River IJ. In return Cuypers gave the
city a neo-renaissance 'curtain' on the
axis of the Damrak. The reliefs show
allegories of sailing, trade and industry,
and refer to the classic triumphal
arches, making the central part a
triumphal arch for transport.

334   *centre* □

Prins Hendrikkade 76
A.C. Bleys
1885-1887   St. Nicolaas

Aisled transeptal basilica with dome
over crossing, on a tall drum. Striking
baroque interplay of lines between
dome and towers. The articulation of
the towers and the main body of the
church is, however, in a dry neo-
renaissance. Important high altar (design Bleys, carvings E. van den
Bossche) in well-preserved interior.
Rear looks out on the Oudezijds Kolk
and the paint warehouses Vettewinkel
(W. Hamer, 1899) – one of the most
picturesque 19th century town views.

335   *centre* □ *(april-october)*

Sarphatipark
J.R. de Kruijff/L. Beirer
Mrs. Stracké-Van Bosse (bust)
1886   Sarphati memorial

The idea of erecting a large statue to
commemorate the 'founder of the new
Amsterdam' was abandoned in favour
of a fountain with a bust (after an idea
of I. Gosschalk). Baldachino made of
Obernkirchner sandstone, Swedish
granite columns and balusters, bronze
bust, capitals, column base, gargoyles
and inscription tablets.

336   *tram 4, 24, 25* □

Amstel 115-125
J.P.F. van Rossem/W.J. Vuyk
1887   Circus Oscar Carré

A building which dominates the river Amstel between the Hogesluis and the Magere Brug. Circus building constructed within only a few months, after an example in Cologne. Roof span seemingly without visible support and a lively classical front elevation. Narrow, projecting central pavilion and a main façade with striking ironwork balcony, pilasters, cornice and attic. Decorations showing grinning clowns, dancers' heads and jesters, by E. van den Bossche and G. Crevels.

337   *centre* □

Nieuwezijds Voorburgwal 178-180
I. Gosschalk
1885-1888   Die Port van Cleve

Highly refined building. Smooth transition between a renaissance upper façade and late Gothic: three-point arches, falchion tracery, Marot strap work (Louis XIV), oak branches woven into the shapes of quatrefoils and falchions (spandrels). On the left the bodega-façade with a bell-gable and rococo front (draught lobby removed). Interior with important tiled frieze (Delft Blue) after a design by A. le Comte.

338   *centre* □

Van Baerlestraat 98
A.L. van Gendt
1886-1888   Concertgebouw

Van Gendt, a salesman among architects, who, if asked, would build in any style, was proud of not having to 'play the artist'. He was the architect most in demand in the 1880's and 1890's. He created a dignified, if somewhat arid, envelope for Willem Mengelberg's conductor's baton. In 1988 the Concertgebouw was enlarged with a basement underneath the whole building and with a modern gallery and foyer made of shining materials and glass (P. de Bruijn).

339   *tram 16* □

Marnixstraat 148
B. de Greef
1888   Politiebureau Raampoort

The tower behind the building is situated at the intersection of three canals – 17th century Bloemgracht and Singelgracht and the 19th century Hugo de Grootgracht – and offers interesting urban perspectives. An example of the solid brick eclecticism employed by the competent duo De Greef and his assistant W. Springer. They built countless schools, fire stations and police stations in this style.

340   *tram 10, 13, 17* □

Herengracht 380-382
A. Salm
1890   Woonhuis J. Nienhuys

The most luxurious 19th century residence to be built on the central canals. A 'Petit Chenonceau' designed in a mixture of early French renaissance style and the Dutch equivalent of the New York Francis I mansion style, such as that of W.K. Vanderbilt (1880). The façade is more or less intact but the interior, all of which was designed by Salm, and the coach house have been altered.

341   *centre* ■

Koningsplein 1
Th. Schill/D.H. Haverkamp
1891   Verzekeringsgebouw Kosmos

Tall, elegant building on a narrow plot. Built as a shop, stores and offices (1st and 2nd floors) and dwellings (3rd floor). Renaissance style with alternating red brickwork and la Rochette stonework. Rounded corner with (mutilated) cupola. In the frieze are ceramic mosaics with arabesques, gilded inscriptions and enamelled lava. Lower front mosaic by H. Elte, c. 1925.

342   *centre* ■

Keizersgracht 455
J. van Looy
1891   New York/Metz

The 1880's and the 1890's saw the heyday of the life insurance companies. Architectural prestige was of considerable importance to them and they settled conspicuously on the corners of shopping streets and squares. The New York Life Insurance Company prescribed a uniform somewhat pompous baroque-classicism for its branches. On the roof the famous Rietveldkoepel **(441)** under which is a new restaurant (C. Dam, 1986).

343   *centre* □

Plantage Middenlaan 36
G. van Arkel/W. Wilkens
1892

Van Arkel in the 1890's may be regarded as one of the more refined neo-Renaissance architects, working in a mixture of late Gothic and Renaissance. Though his fronts are sometimes exuberant or stuctureless, restraint has, in this case, born fruit.

344   *tram 9* ■

Leidseplein 26
J.L. & J.B. Springer/A.L. van Gendt
1894   Stadsschouwburg

Tailor-made for the decorative talents of the gifted J.L. Springer. After his success in London (Frascati in Oxford Street) in the early 1890's, Springer returned to Amsterdam to build the municipal theatre. Due to budget cuts most of the planned decorations were not executed. After all the unfavourable criticism passed on the ultimate result, Springer virtually gave up his career.

345   *centre* □

Muntplein 2
H.P. Berlage
1895/1911   Nederlanden van 1845

The original, picturesque silhouette
was straightened in 1911 by Berlage,
resulting in a rectangular block. Built a
year after his epoch-making lecture
'Bouwkunst en Impressionisme' (Architecture and Impressionism). Many
of the ingredients of the Beurs **(401)**
are already present: flat treatment of
walls, heavy, expressive stone supports, 'honest' use of materials and
sculpture conceived as integral with
the architecture.

346   *centre* ☐

Westerdoksdijk 52
J.F. Klinkhamer/A.L. van Gendt
1896   Grain silo

From Amsterdam Noord (ferry Distel-
weg) the silhouette dominates the river IJ. A modern extension blocks the
view of the old building from the Westerdoksdijk. Klinkhamer designed the
elevations. Van Gendt checked the
thrust of the full silo by means of
tension rods, which were heated during construction and then allowed to
cool. The ends of the ties are indicated
by the cast-iron rosettes.

347   *bus 28* ■

Nieuwe Doelenstraat 2
W. Hamer
1895-1896   Hotel De L'Europe

Hamer has succeeded in giving this
building great stature by the use of
pseudo-pavilions with spout-gables
and pilaster strips – a device borrowed
from Centraal Station. Liberal use of
Norwegian granite and Morley stone.
The detailing is a little coarse and lacks
a clear structure but the building har-
monizes well with its prominent and
picturesque site. The entrance was
moved during extension work in
1911.

348   *centre* ☐

Keizersgracht 440
W. Hamer
1897   Confectieatelier Van de Waal

Striking building, especially because of the daringly large windows necessary for the work areas. On the ground-floor base with recessed pilaster shafts, there are smooth, rusticated and Doric columns flanking the entrance. The windows are set between 'bi-coloured' lisenes which are broken by stone decorations and end in robust orbed pinnacles set on segmental pediments above the cornice.

349   *centre* □

Haarlemmerweg 363-367
A. Salm
1897   Ontvangstgebouw Vredenhof

Built in Salm's villa style – here crowned with a turret, such as, for example, Villa Corvin (Hilversum) or Ma Retraite (Zeist). Distinguished, staggered building elements, each with its own roof and a plan for the most part symmetrical. Influences from both oriental sources and the English 'country house' style are detectable. The rough-cast rendering may be of a later date.

350   *tram 10/bus 18* □

Nieuwezijds Voorburgwal 182
C.H. Peters
1895-1899   Hoofdpostkantoor

Derived from the late Gothic Kanselarij in Leeuwarden, this is Peters's largest, if not his most subtle building in the 'post office Gothic' style. Cumbersome when viewed frontally, the building's main volume seems lighter viewed from an acute angle and has a dynamic silhouette. Heavy tower over the loading-bay at the southwest corner. The main hall with galleries and fine colouring is worth a visit. In 1991 the interior was converted in a shopping centre by H. Ruyssenaars.

351   *centre* □

Raadhuisstraat 23-53
A.L. van Gendt
1899 Winkelgalerij Utrecht

The Raadhuisstraat was created in 1894-1896. The arcade accentuates the broad curve of the street with the Westertoren **(130)** in the background. The façade shows influences of Berlage and Art Nouveau in the wrought ironwork and stonework, yet it is traditional in symmetry and ressaulting of the centre. Crocodiles, predators etc. summon the passer-by to purchase life insurances. The arcade was commissioned by Insurance Company Utrecht.

352 *centre* □

Jan Luykenstraat 2
Ed. Cuypers
1899 Residence Ed. Cuypers

An important house in the history of Dutch architecture. Breeding ground for the Amsterdam School. In the house itself can be seen the styles which attracted Cuypers: Norman Shaw and the English country house style, a great deal of half-timbering, an irregular plan and building volume, random placing of windows and striking Japanese influences, such as the swept fascia on the northeast side.

353 *centre* ■

Raadhuisstraat 2-6
J. & C. Verheul
1899-1900   Rotterdamse Verzekering Sociëteit

Insurance companies played an important part in stimulating architects to search for a new style. The emphasis in this case is on new designing and a sophisticated use of materials. Organic decoration on a stone lower front. The Raadhuisstraat entrance has a modest iconographic content. The building is an integral part of the P.C. Hoofthuis **(541)**.

354 *centre* □

The twentieth century until 1940

The period 1900-1940 is characterized by a profusion of various architectural movements. One of these movements originated around the turn of the century in the work of an architect who had abandoned the nineteenth century neo-styles and, so, heralded a whole new period in Dutch architecture: Hendrik Petrus Berlage. Berlage advocated an honest and pure architecture. This entailed that structure should be expressed and that ornament should be confined to a supportive role. In spite of this rational approach to architecture, Berlage commanded a rich architectural vocabulary. This ambiguity is expressed in his use of materials, which were both traditional and industrial, and in the sorts of buildings he designed. Berlage had an enormous influence on Dutch architecture and it is, therefore, highly regrettable that much of his work has already been demolished.

Amsterdam School

Around 1912 an architectural movement came into existence: the Amsterdam School. The word 'School' should, in this context, not be taken literally. As the saying goes: 'for every architect there is a style'. The Amsterdam School was born in the office of Ed. Cuypers, in which the architects P.L. Kramer, M. de Klerk and J.M. van der Mey were all working at the beginning of the century. The point of departure was the individual architect's will to form rather than the function of a particular building. The Amsterdam School is characterized by an unbridled fantasy, both in the treatment of surfaces and in the handling of spaces. No form, no matter how eccentric, was eschewed. The decorative potential of building materials, predominantly brickwork, was exploited to the full. Every detail was used to express the style: frames, doors as well as interiors, stained glass, wrought ironwork and so forth. The ideas referred to those of the Gesamtkunstwerk. The buildings themselves are impressive because of the massive, projecting forms and the frequent use of corner towers.

There are several reasons why so much was built in the style of the Amsterdam School. The Dienst Publieke Werken (Local authority Department of Public Works) and the Rijksgebouwendienst (Ministry of Housing and Construction) had Amsterdam School architects in their employment. The Schoonheidscommissie (committee of aesthetics control) had a strong preference for the style. *Wendingen*, the journal of the authorative architects' association Architectura et Amicitia, was the mouthpiece of the Amsterdam School architects.

De Klerk died in 1923, a tragic loss to the movement. The economic crisis also had its effect: the housing subsidies available under the Housing Act of 1901 were no longer possible and brick became too expensive to be used for extravagant designs. The style was modified and lost its expressionist vigour. The Amsterdam School architects were, however, able to maintain their strong position. Architects who put forward other ideas were rewarded with few commissions.

Het Nieuwe Bouwen

The other ideas were, however, in existence and were disseminated internationally. Important sources were the Bauhaus in Germany, Frank Lloyd Wright in the U.S.A. and Le Corbusier in France. In the Netherlands too a generation was growing up with new ideas. It was asserted that architects should not impose their concepts of form at the expense of the function of a building; on the contrary, form should follow function. The architecture of decorative brickwork fell out of favour and structure itself became all important. New building materials such as concrete, steel and glass were frequently used and were admired for their intrinsic value instead of being timidly concealed from view. Concepts such as light, air and direct sunlight became parts of architecture. A building was no longer an inert mass of brick but was, in effect, dematerialized.

Experiments took place with high-rise buildings and open-block planning. In short, the contrast to the Amsterdam School was total. In Amsterdam in 1927 followers of the new trend, known variously as Nieuwe Zakelijkheid, Het Nieuwe Bouwen or Functionalism, set up De 8, an association which was to act as an interpreter of the new ideas. The manifesto proposed that De 8 was non-aesthetic, non-cubist, non-dramatic, and non-romantic.

The architects Merkelbach, Karsten and Groenewegen were among the founding members. In 1928 De 8 merged with the Rotterdam architects' association Opbouw, and in 1934 they joined forces with Groep '32, architects who had ceased to feel at home in Architectura et Amicitia. The admission of Groep '32 gave rise to problems. Conflicts became apparent, especially with regard to aesthetics. Some architects remained convinced that good architecture is non-aesthetic; others maintained that each choice of form, no matter how functional, is always a choice for that particular form and for no other, so that an aesthetic element really does enter the scene, albeit by the back door. One of the strongest recalcitrants to defend aesthetics was A. Staal, originally a member of Groep '32. The differences of opinion remained irreconcilable and in 1938 a split took place. In spite of the internal conflicts, however, there was, to a certain extent, a collective attempt to break new ground in architecture. These architects did not have many opportunities to put their ideas into practice.

The Delft School which received the majority of new commissions outside Amsterdam, was a conservative, religiously inclined movement which derived inspiration from various traditional sources. One of the most important propagandists for this movement was Granpré Molière, a professor at Delft.

It was not until after the second World War that Functionalism was able to make a breakthrough in Amsterdam.

It can be concluded that the years between 1900 and 1940 were among the most turbulent in the architectural history of Amsterdam.

Plan Zuid, by H. P. Berlage, 1917

Beursplein
H.P. Berlage
1898-1903   Koopmansbeurs

The Koopmansbeurs (Stock Exchange is regarded as one of the climaxes of Dutch architecture. Berlage makes a definite break with the Revivalist styles of the 19th century and replaces it with a rational building style in which purity of structure is supreme and decoration is made subservient to the architectural elements.

401   *centre* □

Beursplein
H.P. Berlage
1898-1903   Koopmansbeurs
(interior)

Here it can be clearly seen how Berlage handled the new technologies and materials. The steel and glass roof construction is not concealed but revealed in all its glory. The side walls refer to medieval structures. The middle columns of the arcade are later additions. The building is now used for exhibitions and parts of it have been turned into a concert hall.

402   *centre* □

Henri Polaklaan 9
H.P. Berlage
1899-1900   ANDB

Inspired by an Italian palazzo, the offices of the Diamond Workers' Union reveal Berlage's new concepts of architecture. In the taut treatment of the façade, monotony is avoided by the 'castellations' at roof-level and by the varying window heights. The tower emphasizes the monumentality of the entrance.

403   *tram 9, 14* □

Leidseplein 28
W. Kromhout
1898-1902   American Hotel

Kromhout is regarded as a forerunner of the Amsterdam School. This is best seen in the American onto which it is not easy to stick a particular style-label. Like Berlage, he rejected the neo-styles, although the style which he developed is rather more expressionist. The popular Café Americain was altered. Annex by G.J. Rutgers.

404   *centre* □

Koningslaan 14-16
K.P.C. de Bazel
1904

An early work by De Bazel in which two aspects are noteworthy: The doorpost-framing and pilasters are expressions of the neo-Renaissance, and the double house is symmetrically planned and divided into a number of equal surfaces. A contrast ensues between De Bazel's abstraction and the naturalism of C. Oorsschot, the sculptor

405   *tram 2* ■

Keizersgracht 174-176
G. van Arkel
1905   E.H.L.B.

A fine example of Nieuwe Kunst, the Dutch version of Art Nouveau. The building is less taut than his Asscher diamond factory **(408)**. In 1969, the Eerste Hollandse Levensverzekerings Bank (Insurance Office) was extended on both sides by C. Wegener Sleeswijk. Now the headquarters of Greenpeace.

406   *centre* ■

Damrak 28-30
J.F. Staal/J. Kropholler
1905   De Utrecht

One of the few examples of American-
ism in Amsterdam. Nevertheless, the
building adapts well to the highly varied context of the Damrak through its
modest dimensions. The expressionist
façade sculptures are by J. Mendes da
Costa.

407   *centre* ■

Tolstraat 127-129
G. van Arkel
1907   Asscher

Diamond factory built in a somewhat
austere Art Nouveau. This in contrast
to other Amsterdam diamond factories
which were built in one of the Revivalist styles. The building is impressive for
the cantilevered high wings. The factory is currently the home of the Nederlands Instituut voor Nijverheid en
Techniek – NINT (Institute of crafts
and technology).

408   *tram 4* □

Joh. Vermeerplein
M. de Klerk
1911-1912   Hillehuis

The Hillehuis is regarded as the first
move in the direction of the Amsterdam School architecture. The characteristic fantasy is not yet present. De
Klerk was here very much absorbed in
vertical shapes, whereas in his later
work horizontal forms predominate.

409   *tram 5* ■

Prins Hendrikkade 108
J.M. van der Mey
1911-1916   Scheepvaarthuis

The Scheepvaarthuis is accepted as the first true example of the Amsterdam School style. Van der Mey was assisted to a great extent by De Klerk and Kramer. The building is characterized by strong verticals and a profusion of expressionist decorations. Now head office of the Gemeente Vervoersbedrijf (Municipal Transport Authority).

410   *centre* □

Van Beuningenplein
K.P.C. de Bazel
1913-1916

These dwellings are given a particular monumentality by treating the individual unit as an entity. Each dwelling has corner pavilions and a clearly emphasized central entrance. The ornamentation also adds a certain grandeur to these dwellings. The decorative elements have an affinity to those of the Nederlandse Handelsmaatschappij **(416)**.

411   *bus 18* ■

Spaarndammerplantsoen
M. de Klerk
1913-1915   Eigen Haard

De Klerk designed both of the blocks facing the public gardens. The parabolic form of the first of these blocks shows the influence of J.M. Olbrich. The other demonstrates the extent to which the Amsterdam School architects were ruled by what might be called 'brick pleasure' in their purely decorative brickwork as well as in the structural brickwork.

412   *bus 22* ■

Dam/Damrak
J.A. van Straaten
1911-1913 De Bijenkorf

One of the first department stores in
the Netherlands to be built in the neoclassical style. The rear extension, built
in the Nieuwe Zakelijkheid Style by D.
Brouwer in 1938, has been badly mutilated. The multi-storey car park is by
F.J. van Gool, 1980.

413 *centre* □

Zaanstraat/Oostzaanstraat
M. de Klerk
1917-1920 Postkantoor

This post office, which is still in use,
shows the extent to which De Klerk
separated outward form from function;
the building as autonomous, artistic
expression. The parabola-shaped window is typical and became popular
among the other architects of the Amsterdam School.

414 *bus 22* □

Hembrugstraat
M. de Klerk
1917-1920

The tower on the short side of the
housing block has become the symbol
of the Amsterdam School. Although it
serves absolutely no practical purpose,
it has the aesthetic function of bringing
the two wings together to create a
coherent whole.

415 *bus 22* ■

Vijzelstraat 30-34
K.P.C. de Bazel
**1919-1926   Nederlandse Handel-
maatschappij/ABN**

De Bazel's masterpiece. The use of
different sorts of brick and stone and
the staggering of the façade achieve a
strong sense of movement. The com-
monest criticism of the building main-
tains that it is too large in relation to the
adjoining canal houses which are
pushed aside by the enormous mass of
brick and stone.
Vijzelstraat 66-80 – M.F. Duintjer/J.
Trapman, 1973.

416   *centre* ■

Baarsjesweg/Postjesweg
A.J. Westerman
1922 4e Ambachtsschool

During the 1920s and '30s the Public
Works Department designed countless
school buildings. N. Lansdorp, P.L.
Marnette and Westerman were among
the most influential architects employed
by the department. The school on
Baarsjesweg shows the symmetrical,
hierarchic plan typical of Westerman's
designs. Unfortunately, because the
traffic situation has changed it is quite
difficult to recognize the original plan.
The sculptures at the entrance are by
Hildo Krop, civic sculptor.

417   *tram 7, 17* ■

Reguliersbreestraat 26
H.L. de Jong
1918-1921   Tuschinski

This cinema occupies a special place in
the architecture of Amsterdam. Some
consider it to be a fine example of Art
Deco while others see it as pure Kitsch.
The exuberant forms of the exterior
continue into the luxurious foyer
which gives the visitor the feeling that,
for a while, he has escaped from every-
day reality.

418   *centre* □

Vrijheidslaan 10 etc.
M. de Klerk
1921-1922

Only the façade of this block was designed by De Klerk. The use of convex
and concave shapes has led, however,
to a strong sculptural quality. The balconies on their different levels have
been ingeniously linked together. In
1936 the windows had to be enlarged
because of the poor lighting.

419   *tram 25* ■

Roelof Hartplein
J. Boterenbrood
1922-1927   Huize Lydia

Boterenbrood was a second generation Amsterdam School architect. The
expressionism of the first generation
disappeared. In Huize Lydia Boterenbrood has tried, without completely
succeeding, to fuse the separate volumes into one. The influence of M. de
Klerk is noticeable in the parabola-
shaped window on the lefthand side
and in the small tower.

420   *tram 5* ■

Henriëtte Ronnerplein
M. de Klerk
1921-1923

De Klerk showed little concern for the
function of these idiosyncratically
shaped houses. His remarkable genius
directed its powers of fantasy to outward appearances rather than to the
user. Note the small windows.

421   *tram 4* ■

P.L. Takstraat
P.L. Kramer
1921-1922   Dageraad

Kramer designed this housing complex
in collaboration with De Klerk, Kramer
being responsible for the dwellings
and De Klerk for the corner element.
Kramer, one of the most original Amsterdam School architects, achieved
here a peak of sculptural architecture.
No effort was spared in the creation of
this imposing complex.

422   *tram 4* ■

Betondorp-Brink
D. Greiner
1921-1926

Greiner designed most of the northern
section of this garden-suburb. Unique
is its village-like character. The low-
rise housing has gardens – at that time
an unprecedented luxury for the working class. Despite the limited budget,
the result is more than satisfactory.

423   *tram 9* ■

Betondorp-Onderlangs
J. Gratama/J.H. Mulder
1922

In Betondorp cheaper methods of
building were investigated, leading to
the use of new materials and techniques. Roughly a thousand dwellings
were built using prefabricated concrete
components. Apart from Greiner and
Gratama, W. Greve – Oogststraat
(1923) and Van Loghem, the advocate
of Nieuwe Zakelijkheid, – Schoven-
straat (1926).

424   *tram 9* ■

J.M. Coenenstraat
J.F. Staal
1922-1923

After a 'Berlagian' period Staal was converted to the Amsterdam School. He was inspired by De Klerk and Kramer, as can be seen on the corner of the Barth. Ruloffstraat and at the rear of this block. The J.M. Coenenstraat side shows a tauter, more personal style. The flats opposite on the corner of the Beethovenstraat and the Apollolaan are also by Staal (1939).

425   *tram 5, 24* ■

Hacquartstraat
F.A. Warners
1924

Like Staal, Warners was also converted to the Amsterdam School after a Berlagian period. The form is unmistakable even though the brickwork, characteristic of the Amsterdam School, is here concealed behind a layer of grey plaster. There is fine detailing, especially in the doors and the chequerboard decoration.

426   *tram 16* ■

Smaragdstraat
J.C. van Epen
1922-1924

Like so many others, Van Epen occupies a distinct position within the Amsterdam School. This block on the Smaragdstraat is distinguished by a rather robust vertical emphasis. Even more striking, however, is the use of colours, gree and mustard-yellow, which makes the work of Van Epen immediately recognizable.

427   *tram 4* ■

Droogbak 1c
P.L. Marnette
1925   Schipperskinderenschool

Marnette was one of the architects employed by the Public Works Department (DPW). The DPW built a large number of schools in the style of the Amsterdam School. This school is modestly decorated but satisfying because of the slender proportions and sculptural forms. *Havengebouw* on the right (W.M. Dudok/R.M.H. Magnée, 1960).

428   *centre* ■

Boerhaaveplein/A. Bonnstraat 30
A.J. Westerman
1920-1921   Badhuis

One of the many characteristic bathhouses built by the Public Works Department (DPW). There is an identical one on the Smaragdplein. Even such small, purely functional buildings were built in the style of the Amsterdam School. Nowadays such bathhouses are becoming obsolete. Will be converted to a theatre in the near future.

429   *metro Weesperplein* ■

Tolstraat 154
J.A. Brinkman/L.C. van der Vlugt
1926/1931

The administration building for the Theosophical Society was built by Brinkman and Van der Vlugt in 1926. The assembly hall with its unusual shape was built five years later. Both buildings are now a library. Despite their common roots these buildings show differences from post-war functionalism.

430   *tram 4* □

Mercatorplein
H.P. Berlage
1925-1927

Late work of Berlage. Originally, Berlage was opposed to the Amsterdam School but because of the disappearance of expressionism in the work of the Amsterdam School and because Berlage suppressed the rational element in this scheme to a certain extent, the distinction between the two became less clearly defined. Berlage's ideas about the design of squares are clearly expressed here.

431   *tram 13* ☐

Amstel/Vrijheidslaan
H.P. Berlage
1926-1932   Berlagebrug

The bridge is part of a complex which also embraces the embankment buildings along the Weesperzijde and the Amsteldijk. The tower, with sculptures by Hildo Krop, is the dominant element. The bridge itself, as might be expected of Berlage, is on the austere side. Decoration can be seen in the use of materials and colours (the Amsterdam colours of red and black).

432   *tram 4, 12* ☐

Ambonplein
J. Stuyt
1926-1928   St. Gerardus Majella

Stuyt, who from 1891-1900 worked for the office of P.J.H. Cuypers together with Jos Cuypers, was the architect of a large number of Roman Catholic churches. The design of St. Gerardus Majella shows the influence of early Christian centralized churches.

433   *tram 3, 10* ☐

Jacob Obrechtplein
H. Elte
1928   Synagoge

This synagogue shows evidence of
W.M. Dudok's influence, but, nevertheless, has a strong individual character. The influence of Frank Lloyd
Wright can also be detected, especially
in the flat canopy above the entrance.
The decorative wrought-iron entrance
gate is a little incongruous.

434   *tram 16* ■

Olympiaplein
P.L. Kramer
1928   Bridge

From 1917 onwards Kramer, now employed by the Public Works Department, designed a large number of the
bridges made necessary throughout
the entire city by the enormous
increase in traffic. The bridges were
designed in the Amsterdam School
style. The actual structure is enclosed
in a covering of brick and stone. The
sculptures are by Hildo Krop.
Amsterdams Lyceum: H.A.J. & J.
Baanders (1920).

435   *bus 66, 69* □

Nieuwezijds Voorburgwal 225
J.F. Staal
1927-1929   De Telegraaf

Staal dit not simply continue in the
style of the Amsterdam School **(425)**.
This former office building for De Telegraaf is evidence of a new phase in his
work. Rationalism becomes dominant;
the transition to Functionalism is ob-
vious. The façade is symmetrical and
balanced.

436   *centre* ■

Cliostraat 36-40
J. Duiker
1929-1930   Openluchtschool

Duiker's intention in this school was to make full use of the sun. He achieved this through the use of glass, steel and concrete, and by situating a low janitor's lodge on the southern side of the site. The result is an open structure in which the user of the building occupies a central position.

437   *tram 5, 24* ■

Victorieplein
J.F. Staal
1929-1930   De Wolkenkrabber

With this masterpiece Staal took the decisive step to Nieuwe Bouwen. It was the first high-rise housing block in Amsterdam, but did not consist of a dull stacking of identical floors. The glazed staircase above the entrance, flanked by balconies is an eye-catcher. This architectural treatment gives the building a rising feeling.

438   *tram 4* ■

Stadionplein
J. Wils
1926-1928   Olympisch Stadion

Wils was strongly influenced by Frank Lloyd Wright among others. Unfortunately, the Citroën building (1929-1931) has been drastically rebuilt. The Olympic Stadium, which he built with C. van Eesteren has remained relatively intact. It is going to be demolished very soon. Wils also designed the post-war Citroën Building (1959).

439   *tram 16* □

Gerrit van der Veenstraat 99
N. Lansdorp
1930

Early example of the rising Delft School. The Delft School shows the influence of Berlage, especially in the choice of materials, but also derives inspiration from Swedish architecture. Later, traditional sources are mobilized.

440   *centre* ■

Keizersgracht 455
G.Th. Rietveld
1933   Rietveldkoepel

The lightweight steel and glass structure contrasts vividly with the 19th century building **(343)** on which it stands. It offers superb views of the city in almost all directions. The shopfront to Keizersgracht 449 is also by Rietveld (1938).

441   *centre* □

Reguliersbreestraat 31
J. Duiker
1934   Cineac

Duiker believed that the living medium of the film (especially news films) should spill out onto the street. The auditorium was entered directly from the street. From the outside it was possible to see the projectors on the first floor. In 1980 Cineac was literally decapitated. The steel scaffolding with its neon advertising – an essential part of the total design – disappeared.

442   *centre* □

Apollolaan/Stadionweg
A. Boeken
1933-1935   Apollohal

The Apollohal, originally built for sport and exhibitions is a good example of Nieuwe Zakelijkheid. The façades, for the most part glazed, give the hall a degree of transparancy. Renovation has, however, ruined this aspect and effectively robbed the hall of its strength. The adjoining Apollopaviljoen is in the same style.
Bridge: P.L. Kramer.

443   *tram 24* □

Uiterwaardenstraat
Zanstra, Giesen en Sijmons
1934

Two blocks of steel-framed dwellings. One block has studio apartments and the other dwellings only. The independence of both blocks is emphasized by the different balconies. Renovations have destroyed the rhythm of the windows by the addition of modern aluminium frames.

444   *tram 25* ■

Valeriusstraat 55
L.H.P. Waterman
1935

On the ground floor is business accommodation, and above living areas. Both have their own well-designed entrances. The house itself is older than 1935, the year in which the existing façade was replaced in the style of the Nieuwe Zakelijkheid – a style which in no way detracts from the adjoining properties.

445   *tram 2* ■

Weesperplein 1
J.F. Staal
1935   Joodse Invalide

This building is characterized by a great transparancy. The corner element with its original crown is the dominant element and is apparently supported on thin columns. The entrance is emphasized by the canopy and a series of round windows. The city emergency medical service is now accommodated here.

446   *metro Weesperplein* □

Albrecht Dürerstraat
W. van Tijen
1936   Montessori School

That this school was inspired by Duiker's Openluchtschool **(437)** is immediately evident. Both buildings exploited steel and glass to achieve good lighting. The main difference is that Duiker's building is situated inside a closed housing-block whereas this Montessori School stands in full sunlight.

447   *tram 5, 24* ■

Lekstraat 61-63
A. Elzas
1936   Synagoge

The angularity of the stone-faced façade with its low-placed windows gives this building a sacred character in keeping with its original function. The annexe has elements directly borrowed from Le Corbusier. The building is now the Nationaal Verzetsmuseum (National Resistance Museum).

448   *tram 25* □

Anthony van Dijkstraat 4-12
W. van Tijen/M. Stam & L. Stam-
Beese/H. Maaskant
1936   Drive-in houses

These drive-in houses, linked to the
gymnasium of the Montessori School
(447) belong to the few row houses to
be built in the Nieuwe Zakelijkheid
style before the second World War.
Their thin walls and light structure give
the impression of openness while their
discreet proportions enable them to
merge into the street scene.

449   *tram 5, 24* ■

Bestevaerstraat/J. van Stolbergstraat
B. Merkelbach/Ch.J.F. Karsten
1937

Bos en Lommer saw the first use of
open-block housing in Amsterdam.
Previous development had always
been in closed blocks. The advantage
of the open block is that each dwelling
can receive sunlight. After the second
World War the closed block was almost entirely superseded by the open
block.

450   *tram 12, 14* ■

Apollolaan 15
D. Roosenburg
1937-1939   Sociale Verzekerings-
            bank

From whichever side this building is
approached, its dominant character
cannot be denied. The tall, slender
block linked to the flattened slab provides a strong image. However, the
building is not entirely functional. The
exterior is faced with stone and the
interior is provided with expensive
decorative finishes.

451   *tram 5, 24* ■

Hoofddorpweg/Sloterkade
Zanstra, Giesen en Sijmons
1939

In this block of flats too great a severity is avoided by bending the corner outwards. This device is also used on the roof, thus giving the corner element as a whole a less heavy impression. Decoration is restricted to the balcony railings.

452   *tram 2* ■

Bernhardplein
H.G.J. Schelling
1939   Amstel Station

Schelling designed a large number of stations for the Dutch Railways of which Amstel Station and Muiderpoort Station are among the best examples. The high level of daylight penetration and the spacious effect of the hall are typical. The murals, which are related to the railways, are by Peter Alma.

453   *train/metro* □

A. Fokkerweg 2
W. van Tijen/H. Maaskant
1939   Nationaal Luchtvaart Labora-
torium

This building, which is now called the Aviation and Space Laboratory, could be called a compromise between different styles. On one side traditional brickwork is used while the other side is in thoughtfully applied reinforced concrete. Pure functionalism is, thus, somewhat softened without lapsing into traditionalism.

454   *tram 2* ■

The twentieth century 1940 to 1990

In the period before the second World War much theoretical and experimental work had been done, which, because of the outbreak of the war, could not be executed immediately.

During the war period, architects from various styles formed a group, the Kerngroep voor Woningarchitectuur, which concerned itself with the question of how social building should be tackled after the war and how to make up the lost ground of the war. Though the Delft School was strongly represented in this group, preference was given to designing and building according to ideas, determined for the greater part by the functional theories of the Nieuwe Zakelijkheid.

In 1945, when the second World War was over, the damage turned out to be enormous. However, during the first years after the war hardly any attention was paid to housing. There was little material and the stimulation of the economic recovery was given preference to: ports were rebuilt and industry was put on its feet again. At the beginning of the 1950's a start was made with housing in Amsterdam. In spite of the shortage of money and building materials building had to be carried out on a large scale and at a high pace in order to cope with the huge housing shortage. Apart from post-war reconstruction an exploding population and a growing economy had to be dealt with.

Algemeen Uitbreidingsplan

The pre-war General Development Plan for Amsterdam (AUP) for the gradual, balanced expansion of Amsterdam until the year 2000 had decided that the centre of Amsterdam would have a city centre function and that new residential areas would be built on the outskirts of the town. In the city centre, mainly offices would be built, easily accessible as a result of the building of wide roads, for which buildings were to be demolished. The plans for the garden cities to the south and west had already been laid down in the AUP. The principles of CIAM (a group of international architects united in the Congrès Internationaux d'Architecture Moderne) had great influence on these plans. Acceptance of new construction methods and ideas about the building of new residential areas with much light and communal greenery, led to the so-called open-block housing in the plans for Slotermeer. After the war, however, the open blocks were replaced by a plan with L-shaped blocks. This method of building was put into practice for the first time in 1947 when the Frankendael area was developed.

In 1950 a start was made with housing in Slotermeer. Many architects were involved in the building of this suburb. However, they were hardly able to realize their architectural ideals because of the influence of the State with its subsidy arrangements. The strong interference and frugality of the State meant that not much was left of the original architectural designs.

The next suburb to be built was Geuzenveld. It was decided to divide the area into 6 large sections and to nominate a well-known architect for each section who was commissioned to design 600-1000 dwellings. The architects, who received these large commissions, were W. M. Dudok, B. Bijvoet, B. Merkelbach, J. H. van den Broek (with J. Bakema), W. van Tijen and C. Wegener-Sleeswijk. The architectural firm of Th. J. Lammers was commissioned to construct housing for special groups. They remained dependent on state subsidies and approval, however, and the architecture produced was undistinguished. The ideas of Nieuwe Bouwen (Functionalism) lost much of their strength when they were translated into actual buildings. The rationality of Functionalism was emphasized more and more.

New materials such as concrete, steel and glass made it possible to prefabricate building elements, so that system building could be put to use. This was faster and reduced labour costs. The strong preference for high-rise building originated from the idea, that in this way space and material were used rationally, and that social services were accessible in the most economical manner.

Prefabricated construction was encouraged by the government in the development of the third garden city: Slotervaart. Since 1954 around 10.000 dwellings have been built. The number of high-rise flats has increased; in the fourth and most westerly garden city, Osdorp, high-rise dwellings accounted for more than a quarter of the total.

FORUM

Towards the end of the fifties opposition grew to the emphasis that functionalism placed on pragmatism. The editorship of the architectural magazine FORUM was taken over by architects such as A. van Eyck, J.B. Bakema, H. Hertzberger and D.C. Apon. These FORUM architects pointed out the importance of the relationship between people and architecture. One should build with the idea that a town is a cluster, a combination of all kinds of parts connected to each other with the casbah as the example to be followed. This view of architecture found expression in the Burgerweeshuis (Municipal Orphanage) by A. van Eyck (1960).

A great deal of building, however, still had to be done urgently.

In 1967 a plan based on CIAM ideas to build on a large scale in the Bijlmermeer was put into practice. Building flats of eleven storeys on a hexagonal grid led to a honeycomb arrangement. A great deal of criticism was levelled at this wholesale approach to housing and it was asserted that other forms of building should be considered. It also became clear that the population of Amsterdam was decreasing. Amsterdammers were not moving into the newly-built areas on the outskirts, but to the satellite towns. Pressure from protesting citizens forced the city council to revise its vision of the city.

Urban Renewal

At the beginning of the 1970's the decision was made to improve the quality of life in the city. In order to reinforce the residential function of the city centre, a plan was made in which building in and for existing neighbourhoods was central. The policy of demolition was replaced by a 'renovation policy'. Half way through the 1970's the first urban renewal projects were executed and in the eighties this has remained an important part of the building policy. Many architects, who produce designs for these projects, are influenced by the ideas of the FORUM architects. They build on a small scale, imaginatively and with many details. Architects searching for pragmatism and rationality, such as C. Weeber and P. de Bruijn, react against this small-scale, detailed approach. From this standpoint the office complex Nieuw Amsterdam in Amsterdam Zuid-Oost was built by P. de Bruijn.

A great number of office buildings have been completed in this area in recent years and new ones are still being built.

In addition to the large-scale office building and the small-scale housing construction of the 1980's, a number of large-scale housing construction projects were also undertaken. A start was made on the north bank of the IJ: Rem Koolhaas drew up an urban development plan for the IJ-plein. Large housing complexes have been designed on the eastern islands on both sides of the Wittenburgervaart.

But the most significant housing developments are taking place to the west and south-west of the city. Here tens of thousands of dwellings are being built in the Middelveldsche Akerpolder and in the market-gardening area of Sloten. Architects and urban developers have learnt from the errors made in the Bijlmermeer. In designing these larger areas, ensuring public safety has played an important role. Variations in building form and the use of colour are intended to help improve the quality of life.

In the 1990's building in Amsterdam can take on many forms. On the one hand, functional, ultra-modern office and business property is being built and, on the other hand, the smallest sites in street façades are being filled up, as part of the urban renewal programme. The selection that follows tries to illustrate this.

Korte Geuzenstraat 98
J.W.H.C. Pot & J.F. Pot-Keegstra
1942   Oranjehof

In 1939 the decision was taken to build the Oranjehof, the first complex for single people. In 1942 the building was finished: 108 dwellings for unmarried working women. The façade, the most interesting side of which is along the Geuzenkade, shows a rather traditional way of building in brick, with brick arches above the windows.

501   *tram 12, 13, 14* ∎

Da Costakade (next to) 158
Merkelbach/Elling
1950   Tetterode

The extension of the Type-Foundry 'Amsterdam'/N. Tetterode, is an early example of the association between the architects Merkelbach and Elling. Merkelbach started working on the extension with Ch.J.F. Karsten however. The building is constructed in concrete, steel and glass and is now occupied by squatters who have set up workshops and studios.

502   *tram 17* ∎

E. de Roodestraat 14-16
G.H.M. Holt
1952   St. Josefkerk

Bos and Lommer was the first area of the AUP to be realized. Together with K.P. Tholens, Holt built a Roman Catholic church, in which the change in church-building since the second World War was expressed. The concrete skeleton, which in the interior has an infill of Limburg stone and dressed concrete panels, is clearly visible. The stained-glass windows are by M. de Leeuw.

503   *bus 47* ☐

J. Bottemastraat
A. van Eyck
1953

The social aspect of these old people's homes was central for Van Eyck. He worked on this project in association with architect J. Rietveld. They linked together a number of houses of a similar type to create a plan which uses the house as well as the space around it as part of the design.

504   *tram 13* ∎

Bos en Lommerplein 25
M.F. Duintjer
1956   Opstandingskerk/Kolenkit

This church in Amsterdam West got its nickname 'the Coal-scuttle' from its characteristic tower. Duintjer's aim was to create a cohesion between the various parts of the complex: vicarage, tower, community centre areas and church hall. The latter is lit by high, diagonally placed windows. Light plays an important part in the interior of the church.

505   *tram 13* ☐

Sam. van Houtenstraat 1-35
J.H. van den Broek/J.B. Bakema
1957

When the garden-suburb of Geuzenveld was planned, six architects were commissioned to build a large number of houses (600-1000), each in one continuous area. Among the buildings in the area designed by Van den Broek and Bakema were split-level dwellings of which the high-rise buildings on the Sam. van Houtenstraat are a good example. Access to the houses above the shops is by two galleries served by freestanding staircases.

506   *tram 13* ☐

Comeniusstraat
J.F. Berghoef
1959   flats

As part of the Slotervaart development, Berghoef designed a number of blocks of flats, which can be seen from the Corn. Lelylaan. He used the *Airey* industrial building system which consists of a steel skeleton, concrete wall panels and timber floors. This offers the architect a great many opportunities for variation. Berghoef built these flats partly over water.

507   *tram 1* ■

Stadhouderskade 85
B. Merkelbach/M. Stam
1959   Geïllustreerde Pers

This building has a glazed curtain wall, on which the windowcleaners' rails provide a certain amount of diversion. The setbacks in the façade emphasize the structure.

508   *tram 16, 24, 25* □

Bos en Lommerplantsoen 1
B. Merkelbach/P. Elling
1960   GAK

The bringing together of the General Administration Offices under one roof involved close cooperation between Merkelbach and Elling (design), Bodon (construction) and Van Eesteren (town planning). This long building constructed in steel, glass, curtain walls and prefabricated concrete floors is divided into two by the projecting central block.

509   *tram 13* □

IJsbaanpad 3
A. van Eyck
1960   Burgerweeshuis

With this former municipal orphanage,
Van Eyck, a leading figure in the
FORUM-movement, built a monument
expressing his abhorrence of functional
inhumanity, to which, in his opinion,
the Nieuwe Zakelijkheid had descend-
ed. The Berlage Institute is now housed
in a part of the orphanage recently restored by Aldo and Hennie van Eyck.
This institute is a new international
school of architecture offering a two-
year post-graduate course. The rest of
the orphanage is also being restored
by the Van Eycks.

510   *bus 172* ■

Overtoom 557
De Geus/Ingwersen
1961

These business premises with their
curved façades on concrete piloti is
clearly inspired by the Unité d'Habita-
tion by Le Corbusier. Originally, Auto-
pon, the garage-concern, was established on the ground floor. Above,
there are five layers of split-level apartments.

511   *tram 1* □

Apollolaan 141
H. Salomonson
1961   villa

This villa on columns shows some
affinity with the Villa Savoye in Poissy
(Le Corbusier, 1929) and betrays Le
Corbusier's influence on the architect.
With a terrace and copious use of
glass, the architect intended to create a
relationship between the interior and
the outside world.

512   *bus 66-69* ■

De Cuserstraat 3
M.F. Duintjer
1963   School

Duintjer was an architect who combined the ideas of the Nieuwe Zakelijkheid and the Delft School. This building, situated beside a canal on the
corner of the Buitenveldertselaan, has
a concrete skeleton with floors projecting through the façade. On the top of
the building is a revolving observatory.

513   *bus 8, 26* ■

Prinses Irenestraat 36
K.L. Sijmons
1966   Thomaskerk

Most of the concrete structure of this
church, which is inspired by Le Corbusier's chapel at Ronchamp, is faced
with bricks and tiles. In the interior,
however, the concrete structure is ex-
posed. The window is by A. Saura.

514   *tram 5* □

Weesperstraat 7-57
H. Hertzberger
1966   Student flats/restaurant

Along the Weesperstraat, which was
widened after the war, Hertzberger
built flats and study facilities for students. A broad interior street has been
provided on the fourth floor. The outside world is, as it were, supposed to
penetrate into the building and this
does actually occur on the ground floor
where the restaurant is situated.

515   *metro Waterlooplein* □

Van Nijenrodeweg
W.M. Dudok
1967 flats

Dudok, in association with the office of Kromhout and Groet, designed a street wall, in which high and low-rise buildings alternate. A fine succession has been created of yellow and black facades and the higher white blocks of flats by K. Molman.

516 *bus 8, 23* ■

Buikslotermeerplein/Het Breed (surr.)
Oyevaar/Stolle/Van Gool
1967 Plan Van Gool/Noord

For a competition in 1962 Van Gool designed five blocks of flats. He was awarded the commission to carry out the plan that was named after him. The flats are reached through two 'gallery streets' within the building volume. The blocks are linked by overhead bridges.

517 *bus 31, 36* □

Oosterdokskade 3-5
P. Elling
1968 District post office

This complex opposite the Scheepvaarthuis has a number of similarities to designs by Le Corbusier. The main building, the office building, looks like an Unité. Most of the halls and working areas are roofed with concrete shells. Together with A. Volten the artist P. Struycken designed the canteen.

518 *centre* ■

Frederiksplein
M.F. Duintjer
1968   Nederlandse Bank

On the site of the former 'Paleis voor Volksvlijt' is now a large bank building, noticeable because of its 17 floors. This office tower is surrounded by a rectangular building of 3 and 4 storeys. The complex has been expanded with a second tower, designed by J. Abma on the axis of the Utrechtsestraat.

519 *centre* ■

Basisweg 52
J.P. Kloos
1969   Reesink & Co

Warehouse with office and showroom for the firm of Reesink & Co. in Sloterdijk. Now houses M & S fashion. As space had to be kept free for a railway, one of the corners of the building rests on columns. The large glazed area in the façade of the warehouse was intended to provide the workers with natural light.

520 *bus 22, 42, 82* □

Dijkgraafplein
J.P. Kloos
1970

The western end of Tussenmeer is formed by a housing and shopping complex by Kloos. The dwellings are reached by means of glazed galleries which serve four floors. These galleries also connect the blocks.

521 *tram 1* □

Singel 428
A. Cahen/J.P.H.C. Girod
1970

Built as an infill on a site in the existing canal façade, this property was designed in precast concrete elements. Great attention was paid, however, to fitting the building into its historic context with regard to scale and articulation.

522 *centre* ■

Badhuisweg
A. Staal
1971   Overhoeks Shell

The new Shell research laboratory was built on the north side of the IJ with extensive use of plastic building materials. The most striking characteristic is, however, the tower, built on piloti and situated diagonally to the bank of the river IJ.

523 *bus 39, ferry* ■

De Boelelaan 1105
Architectengroep '69
1973   Vrije Universiteit

The main building, which accommodates a great number of general facilities, the humanities and social sciences, is largely built of concrete. The façade of the sixteen-storeyed tower are given relief by the balcony constructions that run round the entire building. Several floors are taken up by a restaurant.

524 *bus 26, 65* □

Bickersgracht 210-218
P. de Ley/J. van den Bout
1975

After the war Bickerseiland was scheduled for the building of business premises. In 1970 protest actions were
started by the residents. The result was
that part of the island was reserved for
housing. De Ley and Van den Bout
designed eighteen deep houses, with
lighting effected by means of light
wells.

525 *centre* ■

Johan Huizingalaan 265
L + N architects
1976   IBM

IBM head office in the Netherlands
built of reinforced concrete, with striking façades of aluminium elements
with glazed or white panels. The conference rooms, mainly on the fourth
and sixth floors, are made visible by
means of constrictions in the sculptural
façade.

526 *bus 143, 144* ■

Oude Schans 3
H. Zeinstra
1977

Zeinstra has completed many infill
projects in existing street and canal
façades. With regard to scale and
proportion, his own house fits in well
between the canal houses. The façade
is, in fact, made up of two screens, the
front one of which is white and leans
forward. The window openings in this
screen do not comply with those in the
second, light grey façade. Oriel-like
windows unite the two screens.

527 *centre* ■

Weteringschans 26-28
F.J. van Gool
1979 Kantoorvilla's

On the site of two former 19th century
villas, Van Gool designed these office
villas, of which the ground floor area
was not to be bigger than that of its
predecessors. These concrete buildings, cantilevered out at several points,
were faced with brick and the windows, flush with the façade, were all of
the same size. There has been much
criticism of these offices. Seen from the
Stadhouderskade, the buildings look
very different.

528 *centre* ■

Metro
Spängberg en Van Rhijn
1980 stations

A great deal of protest was raised when
the metro was built, especially, because of the great number of houses in
the city centre which had to be
demolished in order to build it. When
the metro leaves the town centre, however, it runs on an elevated line. At
several points roads pass underneath
the metroline.

529 *metro* □

Plantage Middenlaan 33
A. van Eyck
1981 Hubertushuis

St. Hubertus Society's reception and
advisory centre for single parents and
their children accommodated in the
so-called Moederhuis, consisting partly of a 19th century building and partly
of a new building. The old and the new
parts are connected by a transparent
staircase and united both inside and
outside by a rich use of colour. The
architect intended that this house, in
which the small scale and richness of
detail are noteworthy, should above all
be well adapted to the users and
emphasize humaneness.

530 *tram 9* ■

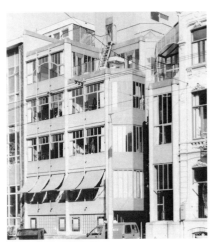

Prinsengracht 151
S. Soeters
1980

In 1850 two warehouses were converted into a school: Louise-Bewaarschool (I. Warnsinck). They were provided with a new, eclectic façade, typical of the middle of the 19th century. When the entire building was rebuilt in 1978-1980, this façade was retained and now works as a free-standing screen. Seven houses and a courtyard were built behind the façade. The hall disappeared to make way for a light well. The façade was painted salmon-pink.

531   *centre* ■

Academisch Medisch Centrum
Duintjer/Istha/Kramer/Van Willigen/
Van Mourik
1981

The AMC, built to replace a number of hospitals in the city centre, also houses the medical faculties of Amsterdam University. The interior of the large complex is especially interesting; an entire city with interior streets and squares, covered by rooflights. As well as terraces, restaurants and shops the AMC provides accommodation for a large collection of modern art.

532   *metro Holendrecht* □

Europaplein
A. Bodon
1981   RAI

The first part of this exhibition complex was built in 1961. Several extensions have been built, the last of which in 1981, resulted in a series of light and functional-looking halls. The external walls are made up of solid and glazed horizontal bands above which is a sloping plane of translucent panelling which is sometimes its own white colour and sometimes the reflected blue of the sky.

533   *tram 4* □

Nieuwe Houttuinen
H. Hertzberger/A. van Herk/K. Nagelkerke
1982

This site, which was originally scheduled for a four-lane highway has been designed by several different architects. The dwellings with their fronts facing into the internal street and their backs facing the Houttuinen are by Hertzberger. The blocks by Van Herk and Nagelkerke are on the opposite side of this street. They have plastered insulation over a concrete frame and brickwork infill. The point-block was designed by EGM.

534   *centre* ■

IJ-plein
R. Koolhaas
1982   Plan

O.M.A. (Office for Metropolitan Architecture) was commissioned to design the lay-out of the former ADM shipyard site, situated on the north bank of the river IJ. In association with J. Voorberg, Koolhaas created a pattern of villa-like blocks, in combination with strip-blocks. The further development of this plan was left to the individual architects. Especially noteworthy are the stuccoed, urban villas by Van Meer. The two strip-blocks were designed by Architectengroep '69.

535   *ferry/bus 38, 39* □

Zuiderkerkhof/St. Antoniesbreestraat
H. Hagenbeek/Th. Bosch
1983-1984   Pentagon

For this site, under which the metro runs, Bosch designed a housing complex in the form of a pentagon. Next to the 'Pentagon' is an archway leading to the Zuiderkerkhof (churchyard of the Zuiderkerk). This pleasant square and the surrounding housing were designed by Hagenbeek.

536   *centre (square)* □

W. Witsenstraat 12-14
H. Hertzberger
1983   Apollo scholen

Grouped round a communal square are
three schools whose villa-like appearance enables them to harmonize with
their surroundings. The Montessori
School and the Willemspark School,
both in concrete blockwork, are by
Hertzberger. The third school is by Van
de Pol. The two Hertzberger schools
have an identical basic shape which
consists of a square with classrooms in
the four corners grouped round a central hall. Variations in detailing and in
the positions of the windows give each
school its own identity.

537   *bus 66, 89* ■

Nicolaas Beetsstraat 82
S. Soeters
1983   Babytempel/Borgheem

Day nursery with ten dwellings on the
upper floors. Striking use of pastel-
tinted brick courses. Round the corner
in the Borgerstraat is a separate building for babies in the form of a temple.
The two buildings are linked by a glazed corridor.

538   *tram 17* ■

Zwanenburgwal
P. de Ley/F. Roos
1984

De Ley, while improving a dilapidated
section of the Zwanenburgwal opposite the Stopera **(548)**, has tried to
preserve the character of the old canal
front. The scheme involved restoration
and conversion as well as new building. The stuccoed façades are important elements in the design. Especially
the block on the corner of the Staalstraat, which is built around a courtyard, offers a stimulating play of rendered surfaces.

539   *centre* ■

J. Catskade 64
De Kat en Peek/H. Zeinstra
1984

The five-storeyed block on the J. Catskade, designed by H. Zeinstra, is set at
an acute angle with the façade on the
Wittenstraat which decreases from
four to two storeys. At the corner the
two blocks merge into each other and
are linked by a striking little building
through which the ends of the access
galleries project.

540 *tram 10* ■

Spuistraat
Th. Bosch
1984   P.C. Hoofthuis

Bosch designed a building known as
the P.C. Hoofthuis which follows the
building-lines of both the Spuistraat
and the Singel. The Witte Huis **(354)**
has been skilfully absorbed into the
design by means of similarities in size
and colour. Giving priority to the func-
tionality of the building has resulted in
the clarity of the design.

541 *centre* □

Bijlmermeer
P. Haffmans
1984   Taibah Moskee

This mosque, standing between Kruit-
berg. Kleiburg, Klieverink and Kempe-
ring, is clearly recognizable as such,
with a minaret on each corner of the
cube-like volume. The doors and some
of the windows as well as the dome
have been treated in a dark shade of
turquoise.

542 *metro Kraaiennest* ■

Venserpolder
C. Weeber
1984   Plan

This plan, which Weeber designed for 3800 dwellings in the Venserpolder was further worked out by different architects in accordance with definite guidelines. The block which is divided into horizontal layers and decorated with a number 1, is by Weeber himself. The block which follows the curve of the railway along the A. Dumaslaan is by H. van Meer.

543 *metro Venserpolder* ■

Strawinksylaan
G. de Klerk/P. Selle
1985   World Trade Centre

This large, blue, light-reflecting office complex consists of four towers which stand on a shared base. The concrete frame is not revealed as the glass in the monumental curtain walls is exploited for its reflecting quality. The interiors are by several different architects.

544   *tram 5* □

Foppingadreef
P. de Bruijn
1985   Nieuw Amsterdam

The façades of this symmetrically designed office complex, known as Nieuw Amsterdam, are constructed from strikingly coloured panels: crimson, metallic and dark blue. By extending two of its wings towards the Bijlmer Station a square is created in front of the station.

545   *metro Bijlmer* □

Sloterdijk Station
H. Reijnders
1986   station

A number of new stations were necessitated by the new orbital railway-line around Amsterdam. The design for Sloterdijk by Reijnders makes dramatic use of glass, steel and plastics. The station building and concourse are covered by a steel structure which floats like a tabletop above the buildings. The railway lines are on different levels. Reijnders has used several post-modern elements.

546   *train/tram 12, 14* □

Ambonplein
H. Hertzberger
1986   De Evenaar

This freestanding primary school is conspicuous in the midst of the local brickwork housing for its colour and use of materials. It consists of three layers and has curved façades with much glass. In the heart of the building is a meeting area.

547   *tram 3* ■

Waterlooplein
W. Holzbauer/C. Dam/B. Bijvoet
1986/1987   Stadhuis/Muziektheater

In 1968 Holzbauer won the competition for a new city hall in Amsterdam. An opera building was being planned for another site in the city. Both projects were undergoing difficulties and in 1979 the idea arose of combining the two buildings. Thus, the 'Stopera' was built on the banks of the river Amstel; probably the most controversial building in Amsterdam for centuries.

548   *centre* □

Foppingadreef/Hoogoorddreef
A. Alberts/M. van Huut
1987 NMB

The head office of the Nederlandse Middenstandsbank was designed from the anthroposophical point of departure that states that nature provides the example to be followed by architecture. The result is an S-shaped complex of linked, brick-clad, concrete towers. The pentagon is an important element in this energy-saving building. Right angles hardly occur. The contrast with Nieuw Amsterdam **(545)** is complete.

549 *metro Bijlmer* □

Foppingadreef
J. Boot
1987 AMRO

The building consists of Y-shaped towers. Apart from the head offices of the AMRO bank, space has also been provided for other activities including a restaurant, shop, café and kitchen. The light façade is constructed of precast concrete elements in which glazed tiles have been set.

550 *metro Bijlmer* □

Hoogoorddreef
Witt en Van Well
1986-1988 Centrepoint

Another eye-catching edifice in this area of prestige offices, Centrepoint consists of two towers, each having a triangular groundplan. The glass curtain lend a business-like air to the complex.

551 *metro Bijlmer* □

Realengracht/Vierwindenstraat
L. Lafour and R. Wijk
1989

This project won Lafour and Wijk the Merkelbach Prize in 1991. Based on a nineteenth-century example, this complex of 66 dwellings is built around a courtyard. This large inner garden can only be reached from a few gateways; the garden is really only intended for the residents. At the Realengracht the new housing complex joins up with a warehouse 12.5 metres deep. It is also connected to existing buildings on the Vierwindenstraat. The façades appear to undulate and the effect is one of variation.

552 *centre* ■

Haarlemmer Houttuinen
R. Uytenhaak
1989

A motorway was once planned here, but the fight for housing has been won by the neighbourhood. This housing complex, with its 93 dwellings and an underground car park, is situated alongside the railway, close to Central Station. The noise from the trains and cars made it necessary to build an acoustic screen. Uytenhaak therefore designed a mock façade on the north side of the complex in order to dampen the sound of the traffic. The 'head' of the building is higher and seems to suggest a ship.

553 *centre* ■

Rokin 99
M. van Schijndel
1990 Oudhof

A greenish-blue tympanum of anodized aluminium crowns the façade of this 'postmodern' office block. It reflects vaguely the triangular roof of the neighbouring block, but is more a reference to Italian architecture. The granite, in red-brown, white and green, comes from Baveno, near Lake Maggiore. The door handles are in the form of two snakes, a reference to the staff of Mercury, the god of trade, and therefore to those using this office block: stockbrokers.

554 *centre* ■

The 1990s

The architecture of the 1990s is in many respects an elaboration on that of the 1980s. Dutch, and thus Amsterdam, architecture has generally continued along the lines of the modern tradition. The influence of movements like post-modernism has been limited to 'incidents' such as Mart van Schijndel's 'Oudhof' office building, the houses on Kerkstraat by Sjoerd Soeters, and the housing complex 'De Liefde' by Charles Vandenhove.

In a few other respects, however, the architecture of the 1990s has distinguished itself from that of previous decades. The past few years have seen the frequent use of contrasting materials in façades. In their design for a building for the city's Public Works Department, Claus & Kaan have created two very different façades: the façade along the street is faced with natural stone and has a formal, dignified character; the rear façade is constructed from steel and glass and is thus much more informal. In their housing block in Vespuccistraat, Meyer & Van Schooten combine a brick façade with a steel construction, thus creating something thoroughly modern in appearance. Paul Dijkman has done something similar in Hazenstraat, combining wooden façade elements with a steel skeleton.

More and more buildings are being given façades consisting of different elements which shift in relation to one another. As a result, the building's 'skin' seems to be detached from the rest. Good examples of this can be seen in the work of Rudy Uytenhaak and Ben van Berkel.

Because of the acute shortage of housing in Amsterdam, the emphasis in new building continues to be on housing. The demand for houses means that most free locations, both those that have become available in the city and those resulting from the city's expansion towards the periphery, are earmarked for housing development. Recent examples of new housing development in the city are the Werfterrein (completed by Lafour & Wijk), the Oranje Nassaukazerneterrein (Atelier Pro), Koningin Wilhelminaplein (Uytenhaak, De Architekten Cie) and the Heinekenterrein (De Jong Hoogveld De Kat). A significant housing-development project on Amsterdam's periphery is Nieuw-Sloten. The starting point here was the need for high-density, low-rise housing. Within the framework of the urban design plan for Nieuw-Sloten a large number of different architects have designed housing for the area (including Rudy Uytenhaak, Sjoerd Soeters, Atelier Pro, Duinker & Van der Torre, Ben Loerakker, Koen van Velsen, Lafour & Wijk and Hans Ruijssenaars). Because so many architects have experimented with different types of housing, a sort of housing showroom has been created.

Another location on the periphery where large-scale housing development is taking place is the Oostelijk Havengebied. An enormous number of dwellings are being built here, to designs by various architects. The urban design plan for KNSM-eiland envisaged the construction of various superblocks; the superblock had once again become an important element in urban design. The most striking example of these superblocks is 'Piraeus', by the German architects Hans Kollhoff and Christian Rapp. The block lies like a colossal ship at the entrance to the peninsula. The dark-brick façades have been kept flat by avoiding balconies on the south side and using walled-in conservatories instead. The small infills in the city are the very opposite of these housing superblocks. Even after the large-scale urban-renewal projects in Amsterdam's inner city in the 1970s and '80s, there were still small locations left undeveloped. The plots are usually so small that developing them is not commercially viable for investors; it is for individuals however. Examples of these modest contributions to the city's urban renewal can be found in the infills by Hans Wagner in Vinkenstraat and Johan Nust on Recht Boomssloot.

Office building in Amsterdam has been given renewed impetus with the arrival of Tripolis. The architects, Aldo and Hannie van Eyck, took as their starting point the need to ensure that the complex should not dominate too much over the neighbouring Burgerweeshuis (designed by van Eyck in 1960, see **510**). The result is an office complex consisting of different buildings with different heights. By facing the façade with wood and giving each element a different colour, a friendly complex has been created which, in its own way, provides a counterweight to the reflecting façades of other, neighbouring office buildings.

A relatively new phenomenon in the past few years is high-rise. High-rise is being increasingly used to provide urban beacons in residential districts: the 'Skydome' tower on KNSM-eiland (to a design by Wiel Arets) and the towers in the Middenveldsche Akerpolder (Tangram Architecten) and Nieuw-Sloten (Atelier Pro) extension districts are examples. Over the past few years major projects have been realized on the periphery of the city too, with very little contentious opposition. One example is the new Ajax Stadium in Amsterdam-Zuidoost. It was not until the roof trusses were added that it became clear how high the structure would be and thus how much the stadium would influence the urban skyline. An even clearer example is Rembrandt Tower. At 135 metres this office block (completed in 1994) is the tallest building in the city. There was virtually no discussion about its height, despite the fact it can be seen from almost anywhere in the city. Perhaps this is partly because the decision-making process in relation to Rembrandt Tower coincided with a heated debate on plans for Larmag Tower. This 200-metre-high tower is planned for Sloterdijk, but it is not clear whether it will ever be built.

In Amsterdam it is increasingly evident that it is necessary to make a choice between preserving monuments, or, for financial reasons, modifying them, perhaps in a far-reaching way. This issue flared up in 1994, for example, when the remains of a medieval castle were found at Nieuwezijds Kolk. Preserving these remains and making them accessible to the public was incompatible with plans to construct an office block and underground car park. The same issue arose in connection with the future of Jan Duiker's Cineac (**442**). Having ceased to be commercially viable as a cinema, the building was sold in 1993 on condition it was no longer used as a cinema. Because it seems unlikely a way will be found to restore the building to its former glory and keep it open to the public as a cinema, plans have been drawn up to convert it into a film-theme restaurant. It is feared that changing the building's function will compromise Duiker's concept however. In the debate on the future of this and Amsterdam's other monuments, the distance between those urging preservation and those stressing the importance of functional use still seems too wide to be bridged.

Rembrandtoren

Johan Huizingalaan 400
ZZ+P
1991 Nissan Europe Head office

Like a beacon, conspicuous in height
and colour, the head office of the Japanese car company Nissan stands next
to the motorway and the railway. Its
red-brown façade conceals the steel
skeleton of its construction. The high
block is accentuated by a cockpit that
juts out and a 'gap' in the upper layers
of the building. Thousands of dwellings are soon to be built in the market-
gardening area of Sloten and in the
Haagse Weg Park, to the north and
west of the Nissan Building.

601   *bus 18* ■

Stadhouderskade
OMA (Rem Koolhaas)
1991 Byzantium

A number of prestigious projects have
recently been realized near the Leidseplein. OMA have designed Byzantium;
the tower block of the complex accommodates offices and luxury apartments
in the sober light-grey blocks. The
golden 'bon-bon box' is also an apartment. Opposite Byzantium is the Ca-
sino, with its marble walls and glass
awnings. H. Ruijssenaars is the architect. The shops and flats next to the Ca-
sino are by Kees Spanjers (Pieter Zaanen). The new building is combined
with parts of the old prison complex.

602   *centre* ■

Entrepôt west
Atelier PRO Architecten
1992

The peninsula in the eastern area of the
harbour has been completely re-
developed since the end of the 1980s.
The area that has housed the new cattle
market and the abattoir since 1887 now,
more than a century later, houses people.
Warehouses are being converted into
apartments and new developments provide housing for thousands of Amsterdammers. The S-shaped housing block
designed by Atelier PRO is partly built
on piles driven into the bed of the harbour.

603   *bus 22, 28* ■

Tweede Bloemdwarsstraat and surroundings
Cees Nagelkerke
1991 housing

The dwellings Cees Nagelkerke designed in Tweede Bloemdwarsstraat are characterized by metal pergolas that hang above the narrow street (hence the project's nickname, the 'hanging gardens'). The pergolas are part of the balconies of the top-floor dwellings. Nagelkerke designed a series of infills in different locations in the Jordaan. Together they provided forty-three dwellings and three commercial premises.

604   *centre* ■

Stadhouderskade 84
Hans van Heeswijk
1991 office

By using concrete, steel and glass in the design of this office building, which is adjacent to the Geïllustreerde Pers (see **508**), a deliberate contrast has been sought with the largely brick-built development of the surrounding area. The building has a curtain wall. The glass lift tower is thirty metres high. There is a two-storey entrance which leads to a reception area situated in a light court. The entire ground floor is given over to office spaces, which are arranged around a patio.

605   *centre* ■

Sarphatistraat 470
Koen van Velsen
1992 Rijksakademie

Koen van Velsen converted the former cavalry barracks and stables into a home for the Academy of Fine Arts. He took 'meeting' as his point of departure, and transparency and sight lines are therefore central to his design. Two new buildings have been erected in the inner courtyard: a central building (providing, among other things, the main entrance, exhibition space, and offices) and a tower containing a library and media information centre. The new buildings are linked to the barracks by four transparent elevated walkways.

606   *tram 6, 9, 10, 14* □

Pieter Vlamingstraat/Pontanusstraat
Liesbeth van der Pol in collaboration
with Herman Zeinstra
1992 Housing

This housing complex was built on a
sharp corner between a busy thoroughfare and a quiet residential street. It was
decided to give the complex two very
different façades. A darker façade, faced
with rust-coloured plating material and
with a simple window pattern along the
thoroughfare, and, along the less busy
street, a façade consisting of windows
and staggered balconies. These façades
are both connected and demarcated by
a narrow, steep stairway situated right
on the corner.

607   *tram 6, 9, 10, 14* ■

Van Heenvlietlaan 50
Claus & Kaan
1992 Public Works Department

An important element in the design of
this building for the municipal authority
was the need to maintain the enclosure
of the work yard despite a busy thoroughfare and surrounding high-rise
buildings. The building is ordered lin-
early, with office space being located in
the middle between two corridors. The
façades alternate the use of natural
stone, stainless steel and glass. This
made it possible to design two quite different façades: a formal one along the
street, and a somewhat more informal
one on the yard side.

608   *bus 63* ■

Da Costakade
Charles Vandenhove
1992 De Liefde

Charles Vandenhove is the only foreign
architect to have built three projects in
Amsterdam. All of them are in important
urban-renewal locations in Oud-West.
The housing complex 'De Liefde' is
built on the site of a church of the same
name designed by P.J.H. Cuypers. The
building is characterized by postmodern
elements such as tympani and neck-
gables. It also has concrete decorative
elements and round arches above the
recessed balconies.

609   *tram 13, 14, 17* □

Oranje Nassaukazerne
Atelier Pro
1992 Housing

Atelier Pro designed more than 300 dwellings on the site of the Oranje Nassaukazerne, a former barracks. They invited six foreign architects each to design a residential tower along the water. Those invited were (from west to east) Koji Yagi (Japan), Alexandros Tombazis (Greece), Cuno Brullmann (France), Patrick Pinnell (USA), Tage Lyneborg (Sweden) and Jeremy Bailey (Great Britain). Their designs were subsequently elaborated by Atelier Pro, who also provided the detailing.

610   *tram 6, 10* ■

Stationsplein
Benthem Crouwel
1992 Wagon Lits office building & Ibis Hotel

Benthem Crouwel designed a complex consisting of an office building for Wagon Lits and a hotel on a narrow strip along the railway. The hotel has an undulating, introvert façade. The tower for Wagon Lits is eleven storeys high and has semicircular ends. It is characterized by slatted aluminium sun-blinds and horizontal window strips running around the building. The building's industrial-technological character makes it a startling modern addition to the city.

611   *centre* ■

Meer en Vaart
Jan Griffioen
1992 bicycle shelter

Because it would have been too costly to build a bicycle shelter beneath the existing 'Meer en Vaart' apartment building, it was decided to construct a freestanding shelter. It is on three levels. The lower level, which is partly sunken, and the two upper levels are accessed by wide stairs and gently sloping ramps. All three levels are enclosed by screens made of galvanized steel. The curved roof covers all the structure's elements.

612   *tram 1, 17* □

Plantage Middenlaan 2
Zwarts & Jansma
1993 Hortus Botanicus

Amsterdam's Hortus was enlarged in 1993 with the addition of a hothouse consisting of three separate glass-houses, each with a different climate. A walkway allows one to walk through the tops of the palms. Construction costs were kept low by using standard green-house-construction elements. In order to allow as much sunlight as possible to penetrate, these elements are sus-pended from a loadbearing structure that determines the appearance of the hothouse.

613 *tram 9, 14* □

KNSM-eiland
Jo Coenen et al.
1993 onwards

In the past, KNSM-eiland was an im-portant docks area. In his urban design plan for the site, Jo Coenen proposed erecting large housing blocks on both sides of KNSM-laan. These blocks were subsequently designed by several differ-ent architects, including Bruno Albert ('Barcelona'), Wiel Arets ('Skydome'), Hans Kollhoff ('Piraeus', see **618**) and the Wintermans brothers. 'Emerald Em-pire', a round apartment building de-signed by Coenen himself, forms the termination of the island.

614 *bus 32* □

Gulden Kruis
Lafour & Wijk
1993 De Nieuwe Stad

The Nieuwe Stad is a meeting place for five different religious denominations. The building comprises a centrally situ-ated oval hall around which two fan-shaped assembly rooms and small meet-ing rooms have been grouped. The pen-etration of light was a determining factor in the design. Thus the roof has been raised somewhat to allow light to enter. The façades of the assembly rooms are made from concrete panels, positioned as 'scales'. The vertical windows be-tween the scales provide illumination along the inner walls.

615 *metro* □

161

Nesserhoek and surroundings
Liesbeth van der Pol
1993 Trommelwoningen

This housing project is situated on two islands. On the northern island there are two rows of terraced dwellings, three storeys high and situated opposite one another. The inner courtyards are constricted by housing for the elderly. On the southern island are the 'trommelwoningen', so-called because of their drum shape. Each contains seven dwellings whose entrances are accessed via the inner court. The floors have been shifted one-seventh in relation to one another in order to guarantee good sunlighting and a panoramic view.

616 *bus 92* ■

Schiphol Airport
Benthem Crouwel
1993 onwards

Schiphol was provided with a new terminal, Terminal 3, as part of a large-scale plan for the entire airport area. In the design Jan Benthem has adopted the same ideas that characterized the existing terminals (M. Duintjer, 1967 and 1971), resulting in a building with a clear structure, neutral in colour. The new terminal is constructed largely from glass and steel. The building adjoins Schiphol Plaza, which is both railway station and shopping centre.

617 *train NS* □

KNSM-laan
Hans Kollhoff & Christian Rapp
1994 Piraeus

Jo Coenen's urban design plan for KNSM-eiland envisaged a superblock here. In their design, Hans Kollhoff and Christian Rapp were required to take into account an existing building which could not be demolished. They therefore included it, as it were, in their new housing block. 'Piraeus' varies in height (four, seven and eight floors) and contains more than 300 apartments, most arranged around two inner courtyards. The small park is by Mien Ruys, the columned portal ('Stoa') was designed by the artist Arno van der Mark.

618 *bus 32* ■

Amstelveenseweg
Aldo & Hannie van Eyck
1994 Tripolis

Aldo and Hannie van Eyck designed this office complex behind the orphanage van Eyck had designed in 1960 (and which is now the Berlage Institute, see **510**). The complex consists of three blocks of separate towers with octagonal floor plans. The central tower contains, among other things, the entrance, stairwells and lift shafts.

619   *tram 6, 16* ■

De Ruyterkade 4
NS Ingenieursbureau
1994 Traffic control and technical centre

This building, designed by project architect Rob Steenhuis, consists of three separate sections, each with a different function. They grey-blue triangle provides space for technicians and storage (of, for example, the large cable drums for the overhead power cables, which are brought in on trains), the terracotta-coloured rectangle contain offices, and the circle is for traffic control. The round roof is covered with copper and will turn green over time.

620   *centre* ■

Binnengasthuisterrein
Theo Bosch
1994 Information pavilion for the University

This pavilion is on the site of a former hospital and was completed just after Theo Bosch's death. It was commissioned by the University of Amsterdam, for whom Bosch had earlier designed the P.C. Hoofthuis. The architect's intention was to design a public building to crown this green and peaceful public space. The pavilion is characterized by the use of a great deal of glass, which gives the whole structure an elegant appearance.

621   *centre* □

Bastenakenstraat, Nieuw-Sloten
Van Berkel & Bos
1994 Water villas

In the south-east quadrant of Nieuw-Sloten Van Berkel & Bos designed both closed blocks consisting of owner-occupied housing and twenty-four so-called water villas. These dwellings are arranged in a fan-shaped pattern so that they can all be oriented to the water. All the dwellings have large gardens. There are four curved rows each with six dwellings. Being constructed from the same building material, the villas fit in with the closed blocks.

622 *tram 2* ■

Vespuccistraat
Meyer & Van Schooten
1995 housing

Because this housing block was built in an Amsterdam-School area, several features of the neighbourhood have been incorporated as reference points. These include the tower and the use of brick. By placing the aluminium façade behind a steel grid, the dwellings are stratified and provided with exterior spaces which function as balconies. The ground floor is elevated somewhat, providing the ground-floor dwellings with a better view.

623 *tram 7, 13* ■

Kortrijk 66-72, Nieuw-Sloten
Edhoffer & Van Exel
1995 housing
A number of women architects have designed housing on several 'islands' on the western periphery of the Nieuw-Sloten extension district. They are Marian van der Waals, Wilma Kingsma, Suzanne Komossa, Fenna Oorthuys, Marianne Loof, Martine de Maeseneer and Irene van Exel. The dwelling type is based on the traditional canal house. Each dwelling has two entrances: one is a semi-basement-level-type entrance behind the carport, and the other is a more typical entrance on the first floor. As a result, a more flexible use of the dwelling is possible.

624 *tram 2* ■

Java-eiland
Sjoerd Soeters et al.
1995 onwards

The urban design plan for Java-eiland is by Sjoerd Soeters. In order to give the public space a closed spatial character, he designed a structure of narrow streets and canals that transverse the island. In contrast to KNSM-eiland, no superblocks will be built here, but separate, sometimes stacked dwellings. A large number of architects have been invited to contribute to the site: the 'canalside houses' have been designed by 'young heroes', the blocks along the quay by more established architects.

625 *bus 32* ■

Hazenstraat 2-8
Paul Dijkman
1995 housing

This is one of the many infills that have appeared in the Jordaan as part of the process of urban renewal. By placing the dwellings somewhat behind the building line, the bay windows are in the same plane as the neighbouring façades. These are linked to one another and to the façades by means of a steel skeleton. This preserves the notion of a continuous façade.

626 *centre* ■

Amsterdam-Zuidoost
Grabowski &Poort
1996 Amsterdam Arena

A new stadium, 'Amsterdam Arena', is currently being constructed in Amsterdam-Zuidoost. It will be the home to Ajax football club. The design (for which Sjoerd Soeters is aesthetic adviser) has a roof which can be closed, allowing the stadium to be used even in poor weather. Amsterdam Arena is also suitable for major events such as concerts. With the arrival of the stadium and the construction close by of shops, a theatre for musicals and a large cinema complex (both by Frits van Dongen), new life is being breathed into the area.

627 *metro* □

Karel Lotsylaan
Pei Cobb Freed & Partners
1991 (design) ABN AMRO Bank

The American architectural firm Pei Cobb Freed & Partners won the competition to design a new headquarters for the ABN AMRO Bank. It is to be built on a site near the ring road as part of the development of the city's southern axis. The project architect Henry Cobb designed a complex consisting of a number of elements: a low-rise building with offices and a non-public banking space, a ninety-metre-high office tower, and a separate conference centre.

628 *tram 5* ■

Oosterdok
Renzo Piano
1993 (design) Science Centre

The Science Centre (officially the National Centre for Science and Technology – Impulse) is to be constructed in the Oosterdok as a link between the city centre and the IJ. It has been decided to build the museum at the southern entrance to the IJtunnel, close to the Scheepvaartmuseum (see **152**), and to provide access from Central Station along the Langedoksbrug (designed by Henk Meijer and built in 1992). The Italian architect Renzo Piano has designed a museum with a total surface area of more than 11,000m. It is expected to open in the spring of 1997.

629 *centre* □

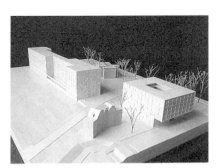

Transitional zone between Java-eiland and KNSM-eiland
Diener & Diener
1995 (design)

In 1994 a limited competition was held for the transitional zone between Java-eiland and KNSM-eiland. The commission was to design one of the series of superblocks on KNSM-eiland (see **614**). The block must both form the area and function as a sort of 'gateway building' for the peninsula. The design eventually chosen was that by the Swiss architectural practice of Diener & Diener. Their design consists of two blocks, 'Hofhaus' and 'Langhaus', and contains 200 dwellings, commercial space, jetties and parking space.

630 *bus 32* ■

Additional lists

The buildings portrayed before are only a selection of the ones one could visit in the city. For the visitor who would like to go more deeply into a certain period, some more buildings with addresses and the name of the architect (if known) have been included in chronological order. The addresses are not indicated on the maps.

Before 1700

Geldersekade 97, 1600
Sint Olofspoort 1, 1605
Kloveniersburgwal 90, *Claes Adriaensz.*, 1611
Rapenburg 13, 1614
Herengracht 84, 1615
Egelantiersgracht 105-141, 1617, Sint Andrieshofje
Keizersgracht 117, 1620
Brouwersgracht 50, 1625
Dam 11, 1632
Oudezijds Voorburgwal 239, 1634
Nieuwendijk 113, 1635
Rozengracht 48, 1636
Singel 282-286, *Philips Vingboons*, 1639
Prinsengracht 2/Brouwersgracht, 1641
Westerstraat 54, 1642
Kloveniersburgwal 95, *Philips Vingboons*, 1642, Jan Poppenhuis
Oudezijds Achterburgwal 161, 1643
Oudezijds Achterburgwal 76, 1645
Oudezijds Achterburgwal 185, 1645
Palmgracht 20-26, 1648, Bosschehofje
Elandsgracht 104-142, 1650, Venetiahofje
Voetboogstraat 14, 1650
Prins Hendrikkade 155-156/Kalkmarkt 2, 1650
Voetboogstraat 22-24, 1651
Buiten Bantammerstraat 3-5, 1652
Beulingstraat 25, 1653
Korte Prinsengracht 9, 1653
Oudezijds Voorburgwal 19, 1656
Lauriergracht 23, 1658
Oostenburgergracht 75-77-81, 1660, Admiraliteitslijnbaan
Begijnhof 23, 1660
Oudezijds Voorburgwal 197, 1661, Prinsenhof
Herengracht 462, *Adriaan Dortsman*, 1665
Leidsegracht 37, 1666
Herengracht 507, 1666
Amstelveld 2-6, *Daniel Stalpaert*, 1668, Amstelkerk
Herengracht 275, 1669

Vijzelgracht 2, *Adriaan Dortsman*, 1669, Walenweeshuis/Maison Descartes
Herengracht 476, 1670
Herengracht 504, 1670
Herengracht 623, *Adriaan Dortsman*, 1671
Raamgracht 6-8, *Philips Vingboons*, 1673
Oudezijds Voorburgwal 246, 1683
Leidsegracht 25, 1684
Keizersgracht 486-488, 1686
Herengracht 526, 1686
Herenstraat 40/Keizersgracht, 1686
Herengracht 464, *Barent Oosthuysen*, 1686
Herengracht 528-530, 1687, Huis Gebroeders Trip
Herengracht 508-510, *Pieter Adolfse de Zeeuw*, 1688
Kalverstraat 100-104, 1696

Eighteenth century

Brouwersgracht 99, 1711
Herengracht 567, 1718
Herengracht 342, 1720
Begijnhof 19-20, 1721
Keizersgracht 158, 1721
Spuistraat 127, first quarter
Singel 320, first quarter
Herengracht 166, 1725, Soli Deo Gloria
Herengracht 479, 1725
Singel 377-379, 1730
Herengracht 476, 1730
Begijnhof 22, 1736
Keizersgracht 137-139, 1738
Bloemgracht 172, 1740
Prinsengracht 25-27, 1740
Herengracht 605, 1740, Museum Willet Holthuysen
Herengracht 592, 1740
Herengracht 274, 1740, D'Witte Leli
Singel 104-106, 1740
Herengracht 609-611, 1741
Herengracht 543, 1743
Begijnhof 33, 1744, Poelenburgh
Prinsengracht 122, 1744
Amstel 86-98, *P. Pantel* (gate), 1746, Swigtershof
Prins Hendrikkade 134, second quarter
Keizersgracht 225, 1746, Koopermolen
Zanddwarsstraat 6, 1747
Gravenstraat 18, 1750
Singel 116, 1750, Huis met de Neuzen
Prinsengracht 1099, 1750
Singel 318, 1750
Herengracht 499, 1750
Singel 36, 1754, Zeevrugt
Prinsengracht 126, 1755
Singel 288, 1755
Begijnhof 40, 1757
Herengracht 160, 1760

Singel 66-68, 1760
Prins Hendrikkade 135, third quarter
Herengracht 615-617, 1767
Prinsengracht 281, *Abraham van der Hart*, 1779
Herengracht 580, 1780 (top floor, 1922)
Keizersgracht 146, 1780
Singel 210, 1790
Keizersgracht 121, 1790
Singel 430, 1795

Nineteenth century

Herengracht 460, c. 1803
Prinsengracht 89-113, *Abraham van der Hart*, 1804, Hofje De Star
Sarphatistraat 154, *Abraham van der Hart*, 1812, Oranje-Nassaukazerne
Prins Hendrikkade 142, *T. F. Suys*, 1828, Zeemanshoop
Herengracht 431, *M. G. Tétar van Elven*, 1841, Kerk 'Bij 't Lam'
Oostenburgervaart (seen from Conradstraat), c. 1847, Nieuwe Zeemaga-
    zijn V.O.C. (1720), converted into factory of steammachines
Kalverstraat 58, *G. Moele*, 1848, Kerk H.H. Petrus en Paulus/Papegaai
Keizersgracht 218-220, *Th. Molkenboer*, 1854, Redemptoristenkerk
Prinsengracht 754, *Th. Molkenboer*, 1857, Sint Willibrordus binnen de
    Veste/Duif
Keizersgracht 493, *A. N. Godefroy*, 1860, warehouse
Herengracht 54, *C. Wiegand*, 1868
Keizersgracht 439, *G. B. Salm*, 1871
Oosteinde 1-27, *C. Outshoorn*, 1871
Oude Turfmarkt 25/Grimburgwal, *A. N. Godefroy/B. de Greef*, 1871 &
    1875, Kraamvrouwenkliniek/Binnengasthuis
Herengracht 468, *S. W. van Rouendal*, 1874
Stadhouderskade 86, *B. de Greef*, 1875, Rijksacademie voor Beeldende
    Kunsten
Keizersgracht 670, *J. L. Springer*, 1876
Uilenburgerstraat 173-175, *J. W. Meijer*, 1878, Diamantfabriek Boas
Weteringschans 6-8, *G. B. & A. Salm*, 1879, Vrije Gemeente/Paradiso
Kloveniersburgwal 137-139, *I. Gosschalk*, 1879
Bloemgracht 98, 1880, Afgescheiden Kerk
Marnixstraat 398-400, *Ed. Cuypers*, c. 1881, 'Maison Stroucken'
Weteringschans 16-18, *N. Vos*, 1882
Weteringschans 10-12-14, *J. Daverman*, 1882-1884
Damrak 1-5, *J. F. Henkenhaf*, 1883, Victoria Hotel
Rokin 84, *A. L. van Gendt*, 1883, Riche Restaurant
Droogbak 13, *A. C. Bleys*, 1883
Kloveniersburgwal 87-89/Groenburgwal 24, *L. Beirer*, 1883
Rapenburgerstraat 109, *G. B. & A. Salm*, 1883, Synagoge
Droogbak 1a, *C. B. Posthumus Meyjes sr.*, 1883, Hollandse IJzeren
    Spoorweg Maatschappij/Nederlands Documentatiecentrum voor de
    Bouwkunst
Czaar Peterstraat 199-205, *J. W. Meijer*, 1884
Tesselschadestraat 31/Vondelstraat, *Jos. Th. J. Cuypers*, 1885, Oud
    Leyerhoven
Weteringschans 29, *W. & J. B. Springer*, 1885, Barlaeus Gymnasium
Ceintuurbaan 251-255, *A. C. Boerma*, 1885
Damrak 62, *J. van Looy*, 1886, Allert de Lange Bookseller
Veelaan/Cruquiusweg 46-48, *A. C. Boerma, E. Damen and Dienst Publie-
    ke Werken*, 1887, Abbatoir en Veemarkt

Keizersgracht 566, *G. B. & A. Salm*, 1888, Dolerende Kerk
Frederiksplein 12, *W. Langhout Gzn.*, 1890
Spui 10a, *Ed. Cuypers*, 1892, Meubelmagazijn H. F. Jansen/Afrikahuis
Nicolaas Witsenkade 32, *H. G. Jansen*, 1892
Amsteldijk 67, *R. Kuipers/W. J. de Groot*, 1892, Raadhuis Nieuwer-Amstel/Gemeente Archief
Spuistraat 12-14/Teerketelsteeg, *P. J. H. & Jos. Th. J. Cuypers*, 1893, Dominicuskerk
Kalverstraat 200, *G. van Arkel*, 1893
Roemer Visscherstraat 20-30a, *Tj. Kuipers*, 1894, Zeven Landen: Duitsland, Frankrijk, Spanje, Italië, Rusland, Nederland, Engeland
Paulus Potterstraat 13, *A. W. Weissman*, 1895, Stedelijk Museum
Zandpad 5/Vondelpark, *C. B. Posthumus Meyjes sr.*, 1895, Huishoud-school/Jeugdherberg
Honthorststraat 25-27, *H. Leguyt*, 1897, Brandweerkazerne
Jan Luykenstraat 28-30, *G. van Arkel*, 1897
Spui 15, *G. van Arkel*, c. 1898/1909, Gebouw Helios
Hobbemastraat 26, *K. Muller/J. Ingenohl*, 1898, VELOX (cycle school), 1911: Zuiderbad
Van Hallstraat 4, *Dienst Publieke Werken*, 1899, Pompstation Gemeente Waterleidingen

Twentieth century until 1940

Da Costakade 104, *H. P. Berlage*, 1900/1908, Koning & Bienfait
Rokin 69, *G. van Arkel*, 1901
Haarlemmerdijk 39, *F. M. J. Caron*, 1902
Hobbemastraat 14-16, *E. Breman*, 1902
Honthorststraat 12, *A. W. Weissman*, 1902, Lizzy Cottage
Nieuwezijds Voorburgwal 234-240, *Ed. Cuypers*, 1902, Algemeen Handelsblad
Van Ostadestraat/Tweede van der Helststraat, *C. B. Posthumus Meyjes sr.*, 1903, Oranjekerk
Rokin 102, *C. B. Posthumus Meyjes sr.*, 1904, Leesmuseum/Sotheby Mak van Waay
Spui 14, *L. G. Mohrmann*, 1904, Athenaeum Bookseller
Herengracht 426-430/Leidsestraat 1-3, *P. A. Weeldenburg*, 1904
Linnaeusstraat 74-96, *H. P. Berlage*, 1905
Rokin 138-160, *A. Jacot/W. Oldewelt*, 1909, Bonneterie
Museumplein 13-15, *J. London*, 1910
Leidseplein/Kleine Gartmanplantsoen, *A. Jacot*, 1911, Hirsch
Beursplein 5, *Jos. Th. J. Cuypers*, 1913, Effectenbeurs
Rokin 92-96, *Gebr. Van Gendt (A. L. zn)*, 1914, Hajenius
Dam 23-31, *F. Kuipers*, 1916, Industria
Jacob Obrechtplein 1, *Dienst Publieke Werken*, 1916, Sub-station
Marnixstraat 266-340, *J. E. van der Pek*, 1918, Amsterdams Tehuis voor Arbeiders
Corn. Krusemanstraat/Amstelveenseweg, *J. C. van Epen*, 1918
Zaanhof, *H. J. M. Walenkamp*, 1918
Kraaipanstraat (surroundings), *J. Gratema/H. P. Berlage/G. Versteeg*, 1919
De Ruyterkade, pier 7, *G. F. La Croix*, 1919, Rederij Koppe
Galileïplantsoen, *J. F. Staal*, 1920
Pieter Lastmankade 31-95, *J. C. van Epen*, 1920
Middenweg 401, *J. Roodenburgh*, 1920, AJAX-stadion

Ceintuurbaan 282-284, *W. Noorlander*, 1921, Ceintuur Theater
Heinzestraat 13-23, *P. L. Kramer*, 1921
Baarsjesweg/Postjesweg, *F. A. Warners*, 1922, Ambachtschool
Plantage Muidergracht 4, *Dienst Publieke Werken*, 1922, Laboratorium
Valeriusplein, *J. de Meyer*, 1922, Toiletten
Holendrechtstraat/Uithoornstraat, *M. Staal-Kropholler*, 1922
Stadhouderskade 1, *P. L. Marnette*, 1923, Gemeente-tram
Harmoniehof 1-24, 32-69, *J. C. van Epen*, 1923
Overtoom 37-41, *P. L. Marnette*, 1924, Politiebureau
Zonneplein, *B. T. Boeyinga*, 1924
Hoofdweg/Postjesweg, *P. L. Kramer*, 1925
Linnaeusstraat 2, *M. A. & J. van Nieukerken*, 1925, Tropenmuseum/
Koninklijk Instituut voor de Tropen
Museumplein 4, *J. de Bie Leuveling Tjeenk*, 1925, Villa Troostwijk/
Museum Over-Holland
Oudezijds Voorburgwal 197, *N. Lansdorp*, 1923-1926, Stadhuis
Hagendoornplein, *A. J. Kropholler*, 1921-1926, St. Ritaklooster/Kerk
Vijzelstraat 2-20, *G. J. Rutgers*, 1926, Carlton Hotel
Hoofdweg, *H. Th. Wijdeveld*, 1927
Averhornstraat 17-18, 23-24/Purmerplein, *B. T. Boeyinga*, 1927
Oranje Nassaulaan 26, *M. J. Granpré Molière*, 1927
Kerkstraat 45-49, *H. A. van Anrooy*, 1927
Amstelkade 195-197, 148-165, *G. J. Rutgers*, 1927-1928
Deurloostraat/Dongestraat, *H. A. van Anrooy*, 1928, Vrij-Kath. Kerk
Linnaeushof, *A. J. Kropholler*, 1928, Kerk H.H. Martelaren van Gorkum
Roelof Hartplein 4-6, *B. van den Nieuwen Amstel*, 1928, Het Nieuwe
Huis/Openbare Bibliotheek
Stadhouderskade 6, *F. A. Warners*, 1928, Atlanta
Stadhouderskade 7-9, *F. Kuipers*, 1928, A.M.V.J./Barbizon Hotel
Aalsmeerweg 56-74, *A. Boeken*, 1928
Minervalaan/Gerrit van der Veenstraat, *G. J. Rutgers*, 1929
Stadionweg 44, *H. Elte*, 1929
Bachstraat 3, *P. Vorkink/J. Th. Wormser*, 1930, Muziekschool/Conserva-
torium
Parnassusweg 11-37, 12-38, *J. Roodenburgh*, 1931
De Lairessestraat 174, *B. T. Boeyinga*, 1932, Laboratorium
Olympiaplein, *G. Friedhoff*, 1932, Van Heutz Monument
Diepenbrockstraat/Herman Gorterstraat, *J. Roodenburgh*, 1932, Remon-
stranten Kerk
De Ruyterkade, pier 10, *J. de Meyer*, 1932
Minervaplein, *C. J. Blaauw*, 1932/1956
Mauritskade 14, *F. A. Eschauzier*, 1928-1933, Amstel Brouwerij/Heine-
ken
Wielingenstraat/Volkerakstraat, *G. Friedhoff*, 1930-1933, Diaconie Wees-
huis
Spuistraat 210, *W. Klok/Gebr. Van Gendt (A. L. zn)*, 1934, Bungehuis
Geuzenkade/Geuzenstraat, *N. Ch. Dekker*, 1934
Kleine Gartmanplantsoen, *J. Wils*, 1936, City Theater
Diepenbrockstraat 15, *F. A. Eschauzier*, 1938
Stadionweg/Beethovenstraat/Cliostraat, *J. F. Berghoef*, 1938, Muzenhof
Haarlemmerweg 475, *B. Merkelbach*, 1939, Firma W. van Rijn

Twentieth century after 1940

Eerste Weteringplantsoen 2, *N. Ch. Dekker*, 1941, Museumflat

Dam, *J.J.P. Oud/J. Raedecker*, 1949, Nationaal Monument
H. de Vrieslaan/Lorentzlaan, *Merckelbach en Elling*, 1951, Frankendael
Van Baerlestraat 31, *J. Sargentini/F.A. Eschauzier/J. Leupen*, 1951, Stedelijk Museum
Korte Prinsengracht 41-89, *A. Komter*, 1955
Wibautstraat 125, *De Geus en Ingwersen*, 1956, Patrimonium/Delta Scholen
Slotermeerlaan 75-101, *A. Warners*, 1956
Wibautstraat 2-4, *G. Friedhoff*, 1958, Belastingkantoor
Museumplein 5, *H. Knijtijzer*, 1958, ANWB
Beethovenstraat 197, *M.A. Stam*, 1960, Princesseflat
Wibautstraat 224, *W.S. van Erve/A.R. van der Heyden*, 1960, Renault
Generaal Vetterstraat 7, *M.A. Stam*, 1961, Waalpaal
Singel 542-544, *K.L. Sijmons Dzn.*, 1964, Vereenigde Spaarbank
Wibautstraat 150, *E.H. Kraaijvanger*, 1964, Volkskrant
Amstelveenseweg, *P.J. Elling*, 1965, pompstation
Weesperstraat 99, *A. Staal*, 1966, Metropool
Weldam 10, *G.Th. Rietveld*, 1966
Drentestraat 21, *H. Salomonson*, 1966, Turmac
Jacob Soetendorpstraat 8, *L.H.P. Waterman*, 1966, Synagoge
Singel 425, *J. Leupen/F.H. Gerretsen/N.G. Mayer*, 1966, Universiteitsbibliotheek
Frederik Roeskestraat 96, *G.Th. Rietveld*, 1967, Rietveld Academie
Wibautstraat 129-131, *Van den Broek en Bakema*, 1967, Parool/Trouw
Koninigin Wilhelminaplein 13, *Maaskant, Van Dommelen, Kroos en Senf*, 1968, Confectiecentrum
Van Ostadestraat 270, *J. van Stigt*, 1968, Hoeksteen Kerk
Noordhollandstraat 1, 3-17, *Pennink*, 1969, Menno Simonsz. Huis
A.J. Ernststraat 869, *H. Hupkes*, 1971, Andries Kerk
Weesperplein 8, *A. Bodon*, 1972, Weesperstaete
Zuidelijke Wandelweg 37, *H. Salomonson*, 1972
Paulus Potterstraat 7, *Rietveld, Van Dillen en Van Tricht*, 1973, Van Gogh Museum
Amsteldijk 166, *Maaskant, Van Dommelen, Kroos en Senf*, 1973, Rivierstaete
Louis Crispijnstraat 50, *H. Hertzberger*, 1974, Drie Hoven
Gouden Leeuw/Groenhoven, *J. van Stigt*, 1975
Parnassusweg 200, *B. Loerakker*, 1975, Kantongerecht
Prinsengracht 587, *G. de Klerk*, 1976, Openbare Bibliotheek
Heintje Hoeksteeg 16-20/17-21, *P.H. van Rhijn*, 1977
Oude Schans 31-33, *P. de Ley*, 1978
Sint Antoniessluis 26-39/Moddermolenstraat 2-24, *Van Eyck en Bosch*, 1978
Palmdwarsstraat 1-23/39-81/16-40, *Van Eyck en Bosch*, 1981
Grote Bickersstraat/Jonkerplein/Hollandse Tuin, *P. de Ley*, 1982
Frankemaheerd, *OD 205*, 1982, Koninklijke Bijenkorf Beheer
Prinsengracht 471-473, *Budding en Wilken*, 1983
Sint Antoniesbreestraat 12-120/Nieuwe Hoogstraat, *H. Borkent*, 1983
Kleine Wittenburgerstraat 104-188, *H. Bosch*, 1983
Madelievenstraat 67, *De Kat en Peek*, 1984
Amstelstraat/Paardenstraat, *Zanstra, De Clerq Zubli, Van den Oever en Partners*, 1984
Tweede Wittenburgerdwarsstraat 4-54, *A. van Herk*, 1984
Nieuwe Hoogstraat 1a/Kloveniersburgwal, *G. van Overbeek*, 1985
Voormalige Stadstimmertuinen 35-39, *R. Uytenhaak*, 1985
Rijtuigenhof 3-197, *Snijder*, 1985
Uiterwaardenstraat 236, *H. Hiep*, 1986, School van Maas en Waal
Lutmastraat 20-38/Lizzy Ansinghstraat 45-159, *Wagner*, 1986
Eerste Weteringplantsoen 40-74/Weteringschans, *R. Snikkenburg*, 1986

Rokin 65, *C. Dam*, 1987, Optiebeurs

Havenstraat/Amstelveenseweg, *H. Duyvendak*, 1987, Huis van Bewaring Havenstraat

Binnengasthuisterrein, *Architektenbureau Paul de Ley*, 1987, woningen

Wilhelminagasthuisterrein, *Zanstra Partners*, 1987, woningen en bedrijfjes

P.C. Hooftstraat 118, *R. Stern*, 1988, Mexx

Nassauplein, *Girod en Groeneveld*, 1988

Nieuwmarkt, *H.T. Wijdeveld* (façade), 1926, *G. van Overbeek*, 1988, Gebouw Flesseman

Keienbergweg 100 (A2), *Janssen & Schweigmann Architecten/ir. R.C.L.M. Jacobs*, 1989, bedrijfsgebouw

Sarphatistraat, *Architectenburo H. van Meer*, 1989, 5 urban villas

Waaigat (Wittenburg), *Architectenburo Hans Bosch*, 1989, 3 urban villas

Sint Antoniesbreestraat/Snoekjesgracht, *Architectenburo Hans Hagenbeek*, 1989, woningen en winkels

Kerkstraat 204-216, *Sjoers Soeters*, 1989, bureau van de architect

Von Zesenstraat/Dapperstraat, *Duinker/Van der Torre*, 1990, woningen

Tweede Bloemdwarsstraat/Bloemstraat, *Cees Nagelkerke*, 1990, woningen

Galgenstraat/Prinseneiland, *Dynamo Architecten/Anke Zeinstra*, 1990, woningen

Conradstraat, *Rudy Uytenhaak*, 1990, woningen

Strawinskylaan 3001, *Architectenbureau Lucas & Ellerman*, 1990 verbouw NMB-hoofdkantoor tot kantoorpand Atrium

Damrak 277, *Architectenbureau Pieter Zaanen*, 1990, AGA-zaal in Beurs van Berlage

Windroosplein, *Fons Elders/Gian Piero Frassinelli*, 1990, Vierwindenhuis

Diemermere 25, *W.G. Quist*, 1990, Hoofdkantoor Randstad Groep

Burg. Stramanweg 101, *G en S Bouw*, 1990, bedrijfsgebouw Data General

Van Reigersbergenstraat, *L. Lafour & R. Wijk*, 1991, woningen

Johan Huizingalaan, *Loerakkker Rijnboutt Ruyssenaars Hendriks/projectarchitect Kees Rijnboutt*, 1991, woningen

Parnassusweg, *B. Loerakker*, 1991, arrondissementsrechtbank

Stadhouderskade 55, *Th. Bosch*, 1991, kantoorgebouw

Chet Bakerstraat (Park Haagseweg), *Mecanoo Architekten*, 1990-1994

Weesperstraat, *Rudy Uytenhaak*, 1992

Bellamystraat, Douwes Dekkerstraat/Schimmelstraat, *Duinker & Van der Torre*, 1992

Hemonystraat/Tweede Jan Steenstraat, *Bart Duvekot*, 1992

's-Gravesandeplein/Tilanusstraat/Ruyschstraat, *Paul de Ley*, 1992

Papaverweg, *Claus en Kaan*, 1993, Eurotwin

Domselaerstraat (Burgerziekenhuis area), *Duinker & Van der Torre*, 1993

Tweede Constantijn Huygensstraat/Tweede Helmersstraat, *Ton Venhoeven*, 1993

Droogbak/Buiten Visserstraat, *Martin Wijnen*, 1993

Strawinskylaan, *Ellerman Lucas Van Vugt*, 1993, De Tweeling

Dapperstraat, *Hans van Heeswijk*, 1995

Prinseneilandsgracht, *Van der Waals/Zeinstra*, 1995

President Kennedylaan, *Claus en Kaan*, 1995 Combinatiegebouw Politie/Sociale Dienst

Amstelplein, *SOM*, 1995, Rembrandt Tower

Heinekenplein, *De Jong/Hoogveld/De Kat*, 1995

Azartplein, *Jo Crepai*, 1995, Wladiwostok

Javastraat, *Hans Wagner*, 1996

Further reading

d'Ailly, A.E., *Historische Gids van Amsterdam*, Amsterdam, 1949
Amsterdam Social Housing Atlas, Amsterdam, 1993
ARCAM, *Architectuurkaart Amsterdam*, Amsterdam, 1991
ARCAM, *Arcamkaart 1995*, Amsterdam, 1995
Baart, J.M., *Het 'Kasteel van Amstel', burch of bruggehoofd*, Amsterdam, 1995
Bakker, M.M. & Poll, F.M. van de, *Architectuur en Stedebouw in Amsterdam 1850-1940*, Zwolle, 1992
Beek, M., *Drie eeuwen Amsterdamse Bouwkunst, architectuurtekeningen*, Amsterdam, 1984
Bock, M., *Anfänge einer neuen Architektur. Berlages Beitrag zur architektonischen Kultur der Niederlande im ausgehende 19. Jahrhundert*, 's-Gravenhage/Wiesbaden, 1983
Bock, M. et al, *Berlage in Amsterdam*, Amsterdam, 1992
Boer, N. de, *Strategische plekken in Amsterdam*, Amsterdam, 1994
Boeken, A., *Amsterdamse Stoepen*, Amsterdam, 1950
Boterenbrood, H. & Prang, J., *Van der Mey en het Scheepvaarthuis*, 's-Gravenhage, 1989
Brugmans, H. & Loosjes, A., *Amsterdam in Beeld*, Amsterdam, z.j.
Buch, J., *A Century of Dutch Architecture in the Netherlands 1880-1980*, Rotterdam, 1993
Casciato, M., *Amsterdam School*, Rotterdam, 1996
Colenbrander, B., *Style: Standard and Signature in Dutch Architecture*, Rotterdam, 1993
Dien, A. van et al., *Nederlandse Architectuur en Stedebouw 1945-1980*, Amsterdam, 1984
Fanelli, G., *Moderne Architectuur in Nederland 1900-1940*, 's-Gravenhage, 1975
Fraenkel, F.F., *Het plan Amsterdam-Zuid van Berlage*, Alphen aan den Rijn, 1976
Frank, S.S., *Michel de Klerk 1884-1923*, Ann Arbor, 1984
Elfrink, R. [ed.], *Berlage en de Toekomst van Amsterdam Zuid*, Rotterdam, 1992
Fremantle, K., *The Baroque Town Hall of Amsterdam*, Utrecht, 1959
Gaillard, K. [ed.], *Berlage en Amsterdam Zuid*, Rotterdam, 1992
Groenendijk, P. & Vollaard, P., *Guide to Modern Architecture in Amsterdam*, Rotterdam, 1996
Haagsma, I. et al., *Amsterdamse Gebouwen 1880-1980*, Utrecht, 1981
Heinemeijer, W.F. et al., *Amsterdam in Kaarten*, Ede, 1987
Hellinga, H. et al., *Algemeen Uitbreidingsplan 50 jaar*, Amsterdam, 1985
Hitchcock, H.R., *Netherlandish Scrolled Gables of the Sixteenth and Seventeenth Centuries*, New York, 1978
Hoeven, C. van der & Louwe, J., *Amsterdam als Stedelijk Bolwerk*, Nijmegen, 1985
Hoogewoud, G. et al., *P.J.H. Cuypers en Amsterdam*, 's-Gravenhage, 1985
Huisken, J. [ed.] et al., *Jacob van Campen: het klassieke ideaal in de Gouden Eeuw*, Amsterdam, 1995
Idsinga, T. & Schilt, J., *W. van Tijen (1894-1974)*, 's-Gravenhage, 1985
Janse, H., *Building Amsterdam*, Amsterdam, 1993
Kessel, E. van & Kuperus, M., *M. Staal-Kropholler (1891-1966)*, Rotterdam, 1991
Killiam, T. & Tulleners, H., *Amsterdam Canal Guide*, Utrecht, 1978
Kleijn, K. et al., *Nederlandse Bouwkunst, een geschiedenis van tien eeuwen architectuur*, Alphen aan den Rijn, 1995
Kloos, M. [ed.], *Amsterdam, an architectural lesson*, Amsterdam, 1988
Kloos, M. [ed.], *Amsterdam Architecture 1991-1993*, Amsterdam, 1994
Kloos, M. [ed.], *Amsterdam's High-Rise*, Amsterdam, 1995
Kloos, M. [ed.], *Public Interiors: architecture and public life inside Amsterdam*,

Amsterdam, 1993

Kohlenbach, B., *P.L. Kramer, architect van de Amsterdamse School*, Naarden, 1994

Kok, A.A., *Amsterdamse Woonhuizen*, Amsterdam, 1941

Koopmans, Y., *Muurvast en gebeiteld / Fixed and chiselled, sculpture in architecture 1840-1940*, Rotterdam, 1994

Koster, E., *Eastern Docklands Amsterdam*, Amsterdam, 1995

Kuipers, M.C. et al., *Jongere Bouwkunst, Amsterdam binnen de Singelgracht (1850-1940)*, Zeist, 1984

Kuypers, W., *Dutch Classicist Architecture*, Delft, 1980

Kuypers, W., *Triumphant Entry of Renaissance Architecture into the Netherlands*, Alphen aan den Rijn, 1994

Laar, F. van., *Amsterdam woont hier... volkshuisvesting en stadsvernieuwing tussen 1972 en 1994*, Amsterdam, 1994

Lansink, L., *De Geschiedenis van het Amsterdamse Stationsplein*, Amsterdam, 1982

Leonhardt, G., *Amsterdam Onvoltooid Verleden*, Amsterdam, 1996

Lörzing, H., *Van Bosplan to Floriade*, Rotterdam, 1992

Luursema, E. en Mulder, B., *Handboek Renovatie Gordel 20-40 – Architectuurherstel in Amsterdam*, Bussum, 1995

Mattie, E. & Derwig, J., *Amsterdam School*, Amsterdam, 1991

Mattie, E. & Derwig, J., *Functionalism in the Netherlands*, Amsterdam, 1995

Meinsma, H. [ed.], *Schoonheid van Amsterdam, een kader voor het welstandsbeleid*, Amsterdam, 1994

Meischke, R., *Het Nederlandse Woonhuis van 1300-1800*, Haarlem, 1969

Moes, C.D.H., *Architectuurtekeningen uit het archief van J.D. Zocher jr. en L.P. Zocher*, Rotterdam, 1991

Molema, J., *Ir. J. Duiker*, Rotterdam, 1989

Nederlandse Architectuur 1910-1930, Amsterdamse School, exh. cat., Amsterdam, 1975

Neurderburg, E., *Hendrick de Keyser, Beeldhouwer en Bouwmeester van Amsterdam*, Amsterdam, z.j.

Nieuwe Bouwen Amsterdam 1920-1960, exh. cat., Delft, 1983

Ottenheym, K., *Philips Vingboons architect 1607-1678*, Zutphen, 1989

Ottens, E., *125 jaar sociale woningbouw in Amsterdam*, Amsterdam, 1975

Ozinga, M.D., *Daniël Marot, schepper van den Hollandschen Lodewijk XIV stijl*, Amsterdam, 1938

Peet, C. van der & Steenmeijer, G. [ed.], *De Rijksbouwmeesters*, Rotterdam, 1995

Pistor, R. [ed.], *A City in Progress: physical planning in Amsterdam*, Amsterdam, 1994

Polano, S. et al., *H.P. Berlage Complete Works*, New York, 1988

Rebel, B. et al., *Ben Merkelbach, Architect en Stadsbouwmeester*, Amsterdam, 1994

Reinink, A.W., *Herman Hertzberger Architect*, Rotterdam, 1991

Révész-Alexander, M., *Die alten Lagerhäuser Amsterdams, ein kunstgeschichtliche Studie*, 's-Gravenhage, 1928

Roegholt, R., *Amsterdam na 1900*, 's-Gravenhage, 1993

Rosenberg, H.P.R., *De negentiende-eeuwse kerkelijke bouwkunst in Nederland*, 's-Gravenhage, 1972

Rossem, V. van, *Het Algemeen Uitbreidingsplan van Amsterdam: geschiedenis en ontwerp*, Rotterdam, 1993

Roy van Zuydewijn, H.J.F. de., *Amsterdamse Bouwkunst 1815-1940*, Amsterdam, 1970

Schade, C., *Woningbouw voor arbeiders in het negentiende-eeuwse Amsterdam*, Amsterdam, 1970

Schilt, J. & Werf, J. van der, *Genootschap Architectura et Amicitia 1855-1990*, Rotterdam, 1992

Singelenberg, P., *H.P. Berlage, Idea and Style*, Utrecht, 1972

Slothouwer, D.F., *Amsterdamse Huizen 1600-1800*, Amsterdam, 1928

Sociale Woningbouw Amsterdam 1968-1986, Amsterdam, 1986

Spies, P. et al [ed.], *Canals of Amsterdam*, 's-Gravenhage, 1991

Spies, P. et al [ed.], *Grachtenboek II, middeleeuwse stadskern*, 's-Gravenhage, 1992

Strauven, F., *Aldo van Eyck, relativity and imagination*, Amsterdam, 1996

Swigchem, C.A. van, *Abraham van der Hart 1747-1820, Architect en Stadsbouwmeester van Amsterdam*, Amsterdam, 1965

Taverne, E., *In 't land van belofte: in de nieuwe stadt*, Maarssen, 1978

Valk, A. v.d., *Amsterdam in aanleg*, Amsterdam, 1989

Vermeulen, F.A.J., *Handboek tot de Geschiedenis der Nederlandsche Bouwkunst*, 's-Gravenhage, 1928

Vreeken, B. & Wouthuysen, E., *Grand Hotels van Amsterdam, opkomst en bloei sinds 1860*, 's-Gravenhage, 1987

Wallagh, G., *Oog voor het onzichtbare, 50 jaar structuurplanning in Amsterdam 1855-2005*, Assen, 1994

Wattjes, J.G. & Warners, F.A., *Amsterdamse Bouwkunst en Stadsschoon 1306-1942*, Amsterdam, 1944

Wit, W. de., *The Amsterdam School, Dutch Expressionist Architecture 1915-1930*, Cambridge, 1984

Wijnman, H.F., *Historische Gids van Amsterdam, revised edition*, Amsterdam, 1971

Wijnman, H.F., *Vier eeuwen Herengracht*, Amsterdam, 1974

Yaki, Koji [ed.], *Collective Housing in the Netherlands, traditions and trends*, Tokyo, 1993

Zantkuyl, H.J., *Bouwen in Amsterdam*, Amsterdam, 1994

Zantkuyl, H.J. et al., *Huizen in Nederland: Amsterdam*, Zwolle, 1995

Index

Figures in **bold** refer to illustration items

Addresses and Dates

The following institutions are engaged in research and/or training in the field of architecture or are addresses for information on architectural activities.

Academie van Bouwkunst, Waterlooplein 211 – tel. 6220188
Amstelodamum, Keizersgracht 168 – tel. 6224625
Amsterdams Historisch Museum, Kalverstraat 92 – tel. 5231822
ARCAM (Architectuurcentrum Amsterdam) – Waterlooplein 213 – tel. 6204878
Architectura & Natura Booksellers, Leliegracht 44 – tel. 6236186
Archivisie, Zandstraat 5 – tel. 6258908
Berlage Institute, IJsbaanpad 3 – tel. 6755393
BNA – Bond van Nederlandse Architecten, Keizersgracht 321 – tel. 6228111
Diogenes, Sloterkade 21 – tel. 6172735
Gemeente Archief, Amsteldijk 67 – tel. 6646916
Heemschut, Nieuwezijds Kolk 28 – tel. 6225292
Koninklijke Nederlandse Oudheidkundige Bond, St. Antoniebreestraat 69 – tel. 6277706
Kunsthistorisch Instituut Universiteit van Amsterdam, Herengracht 286 – tel. 5253027
Kunsthistorisch Instituut Vrije Universiteit, De Boelelaan 1105 – tel. 5483041
Monumentenzorg, Keizersgracht 123 – tel. 6263947
Nederlands Architectuurinstituut, Museumpark 25, Rotterdam – tel. 010-4401200
Openbare Bibliotheek, Prinsengracht 587 – tel. 5230900
Vereniging Hendrick de Keyser, Herengracht 284 – tel. 6249755

Dates

National day of architecture; organised by the BNA (Architectural Association) – 1 July or last Sunday of June
National monument day; organised by Monumentenzorg (Municipal Monument Care) – second Saturday of September